Stainless Steel

A Book of Trains

by David Maiers

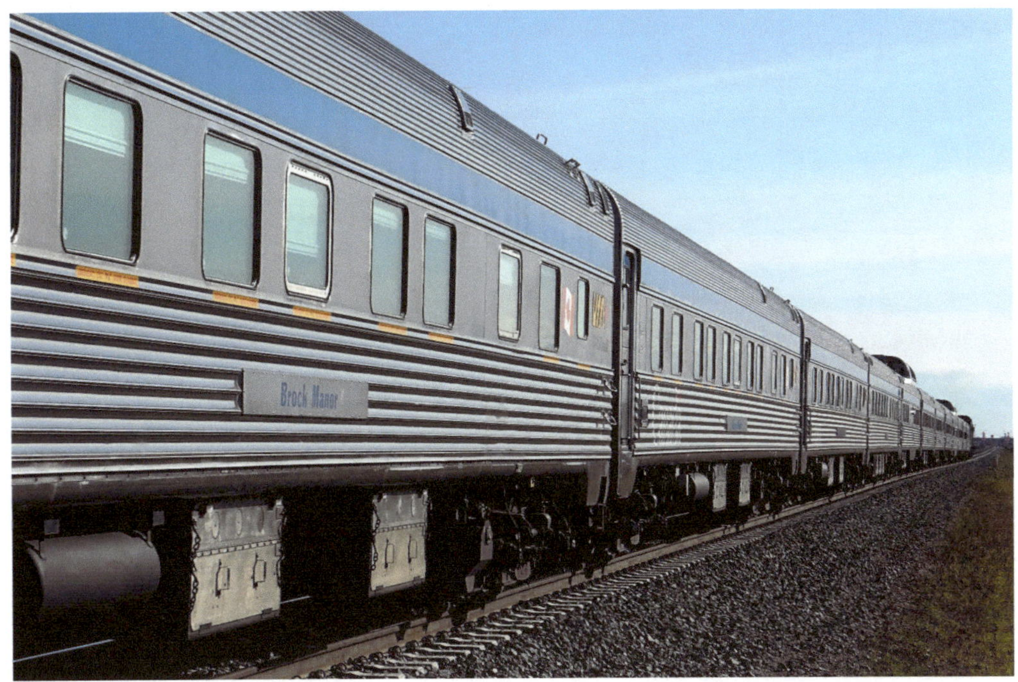

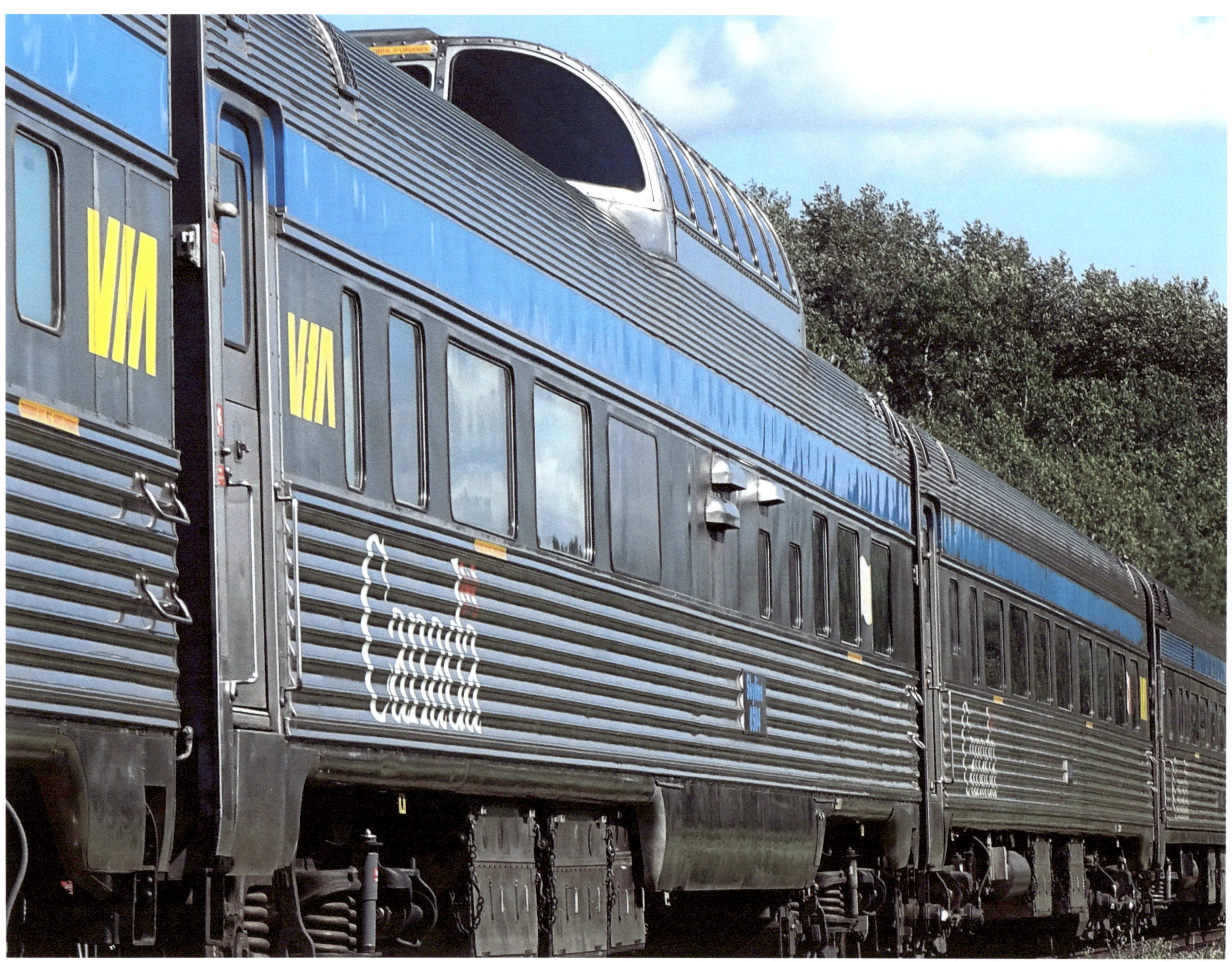

Introduction

Canada is home to the last extensive operating collection of classic streamlined passenger equipment in North America. Coming primarily from Canadian Pacific Railway's roster, VIA Rail Canada maintains these vintage stainless steel cars in tip top shape.

My first encounters with this historic equipment were on CP's western mainline corridor in the mid-1980s. Family trips to Banff, Alberta had us meeting VIA's "Canadian" passenger service on a daily basis at the former CP station there. Train time was a big event at the Banff station. The Canadian was well patronized and the platform was crowded with people. It was the first place a young man interested in trains would see others partaking in the hobby of rail photography.

The stars of the Canadian service at the time were the 1950s era General Motors FP9 6300 series locomotives pulling the train that had just come from a rebuilding in Montreal, Quebec. They were a big deal back then and their classic design was much appreciated by train enthusiasts.

There were night time encounters with the Canadian at Swift Current, Saskatchewan, by then the ex-CP stainless steel cars were mixed with the former Canadian National Railway blue painted smooth side coach fleet. A carman busily filled the locomotive steam generators that heated the train with water during their scheduled stop. The mostly stainless steel consist gleamed in the bright station lights.

And there was a surprise as we drove along the Trans-Canada Highway near Austin, Manitoba! VIA's eastbound Canadian popped up from behind a hill and roared by us on a section of double track on CP's mainline. It truly was a "Silver Streak", just like the movie! My father Len attempted to speed up to pace the lead locomotives but we could not keep up. The speed limit was 75 miles per hour on the track and we were easily left behind! The stainless steel cars were a silver blur as they raced off in the distance on their way east. It was thrilling!

Those sights of VIA's Canadian in the 1980s on CP lines made a big impact. Stainless steel equipment was rare on the Churchill service that served my hometown at the time and it was always a treat to see. Today these cars are a regular part of the local railway scene having been assigned to the Churchill run starting in 1996. This book covers the stainless steel cars and trains that continue to serve VIA into a new century.

David Maiers

Roblin, Manitoba
August 2022 (colour edition)

ISBN 978-0-9737954-8-6

At right

My father Len Maiers visits the cab of a F40PH-2D, the workhorse of VIA Rail's locomotive fleet, a great way to celebrate entering his eighties. Len was enamoured with the General Motors F40, first seeing the engines in service on Amtrak's "Empire Builder" train in the United States. While some compared the design of the unit to a bread box on wheels, Len admired it. He was taken with VIA's initial F40 paint scheme of grey and yellow with blue accents. A 1987 trip to the Canadian Rockies was all about seeing these 6400 series units in action, then only months old. While others were interested in the classic 1950s FP9 power that had lead the Canadian previously, Len loved anything that was new on the rails.   Len Maiers photograph

On the cover

VIA Rail Canada train 692 rolls through an elevated curve and on the rear the distinctive dome-observation car Kokanee Park makes an appearance. The Park car really shows off the classic stainless steel design that was chosen by Canadian Pacific Railway officials in the mid-1950s. These cars continue to serve the government agency well and are integral to VIA Rail's fleet.

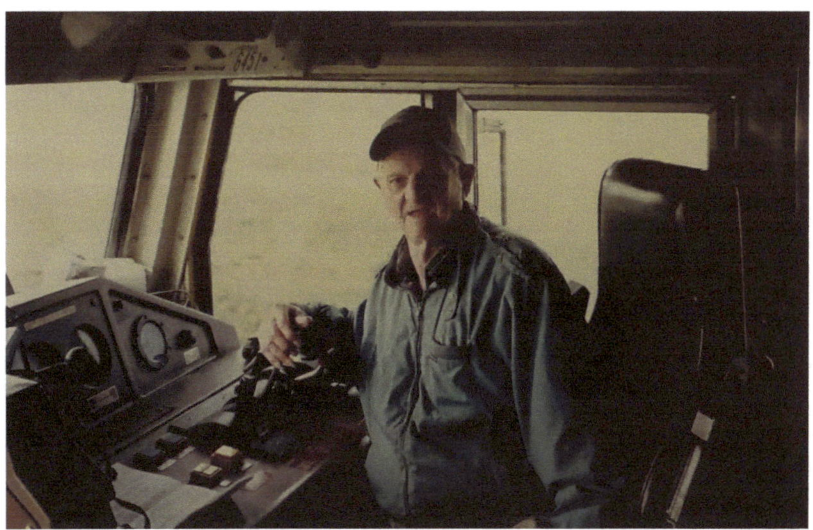

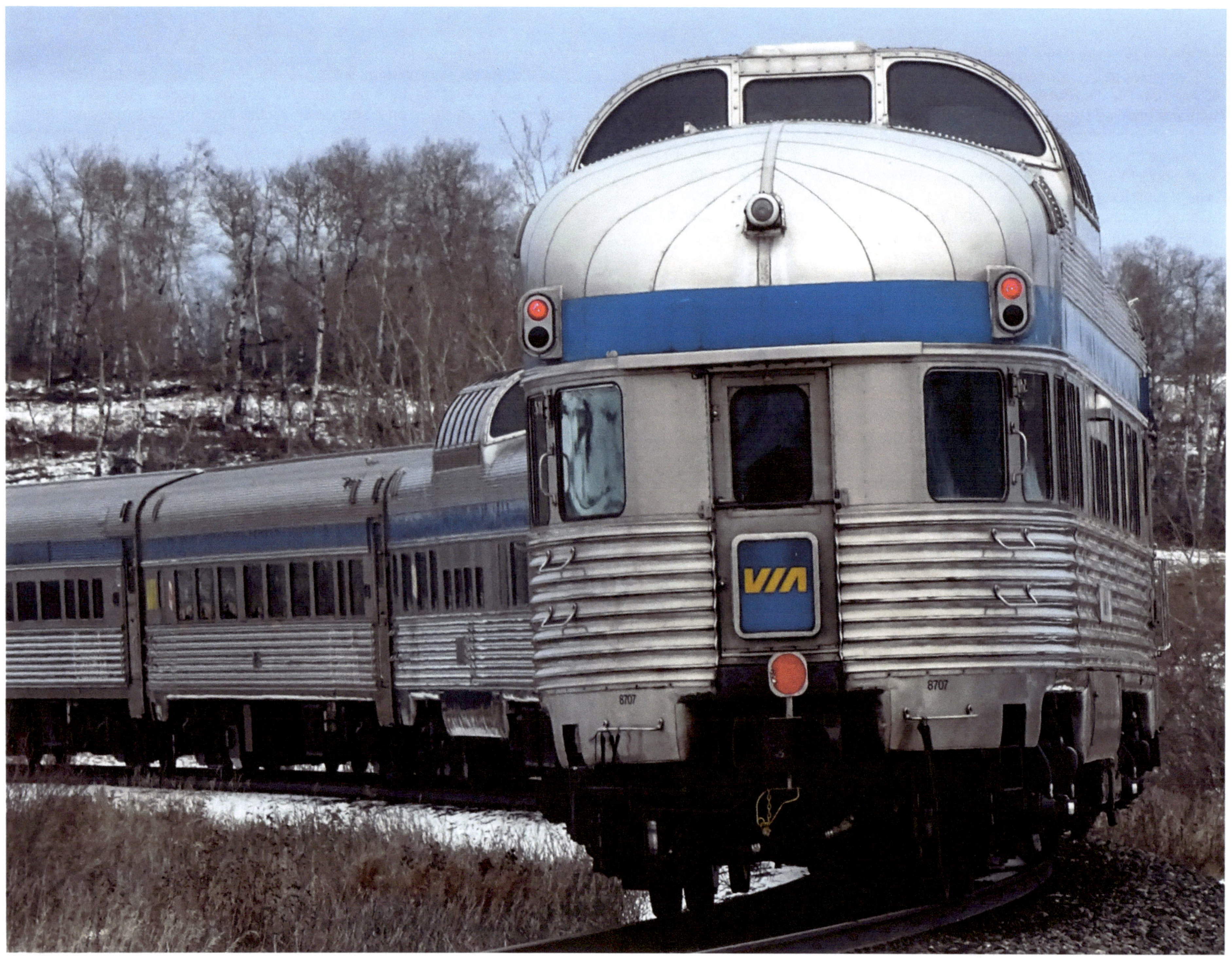

VIA
8707
8707

The Executive and the Photographer

The origins and initial success of the stainless steel car fleet rest on the shoulders of two men. N.R. "Buck" Crump and Nicholas Morant. Crump would become President of Canadian Pacific Railway in 1955, Morant was the CP company photographer who would photograph this equipment throughout his career during the 1950s through 1970s.

Crump was born and raised in Revelstoke, British Columbia, the son of a well established CP railway family. Crump entered the railway at a young age and would later attend university in the United States obtaining a mechanical engineering degree. He would rejoin the CPR and would move quickly up the ranks. Eventually he would be employed by the company as Vice-president in 1948 at the age of 38. Many within the company believed he had been fast-tracked to success having been noticed by CP executives early in his career. Crump maintained a strong work ethic got him there.

After the boom in the economy following the end of World War II in 1945, railroads across North America were being inundated with heavy passenger volumes. In the early 1950s Crump believed this trend would continue and a viable passenger market would exist for some time. Airlines were starting to take some market share away at the time but rail was still being considered the best option for long distance travel. Air travel during this period was fraught with delays and rail was being marketed as a more reliable alternative.

Crump and his staff decided the CP passenger services needed an upgrade and they travelled to the United States to see the latest trends in passenger rail service. They rode trains such as "The 20th Century Limited" run by New York Central and Great Northern's "Empire Builder". It is believed a trip on the "California Zephyr" in the western United States may have shaped Crump's decision to go with a stainless steel streamlined fleet. The Zephyr was a premier train running on the Burlington Railroad through the prairies and via the Rio Grande and Western Pacific Railroads through the Rockies. The CP staff were apparently impressed with the Zephyr's stainless steel design and amenities offered on the train.

In 1953 Crump would decide to order stainless steel cars from Philadelphia, Pennsylvania based Budd Company. This order would eventually amount to 173 passenger cars. They would start arriving on the CP system in 1954 and began service on the company's transcontinental service "The Dominion". Extensive promotion would be done of these cars when CP unveiled "The Canadian" passenger service in 1955. The Canadian was a fully equipped all stainless steel train utilizing the new cars on a 71 hour run between Montreal, Quebec and Vancouver, British Columbia via Ottawa, Ontario. There was also a connecting section between Sudbury, Ontario and Toronto. This would signal the arrival of Nicholas Morant to photograph the new train for company advertising.

Morant had grown up in Kamloops, British Columbia and photography would become a passion and his work. After joining CP in 1929 as a photographer and a short stint with the **Winnipeg Free Press**, Morant would rejoin CP in the press department. Morant would become well known for images of Canada's war effort in the 1940s with one image used as the basis for the design of a 50 cent piece during this period. Later he would go on to have images as the basis of postal stamps and currency issued from the Canadian government.

With his wife Willie, Morant would set out and document The Canadian in the mountain passes of British Columbia and along the north shore of Lake Superior in Ontario. His images of the new streamlined train filled CP advertising material distributed around the world in the 1950s and 1960s.

Although his name did not appear on the images it would help make Morant probably the most famous rail photographer, if not the most famous photographer, in Canada. Two images he captured during the 1970s of The Canadian deep in the Canadian Rockies would be his most well regarded rail images. They would help cement The Canadian as one of the most famous trains in the world.

One shot was of The Canadian at Leanchoil, British Columbia in 1972 near Golden, signal lights glowing alongside the train with mountains in the distance under snow. It would be featured in an American publication and would help attribute to his fame and that of the train.

The other was of The Canadian eastbound in 1976 at a point near Lake Louise, Alberta that would justifiably be named Morant's Curve after the photographer. Morant made many images at this point off what is now known as the Bow Valley Parkway. It features a lovely "S" curve that snakes along the Bow River with snow capped mountains as a beautiful backdrop. This image would be printed thousands of times by CP's public relations department and distributed around the world.

Morant's photographs of The Canadian would draw the eye of Donald Bain who would get to know Morant through work at CP's energy subsidiary PanCanadian in the 1970s. Bain was a train enthusiast and could see there was little historical information on CPR in the mountains. He took on Morant as a trusted advisor and began publishing the series **Canadian Pacific in the Rockies** featuring much of Morant's work. These books would show Morant's images to a new audience and inspire many such as this author.

Morant's work around The Canadian would also go on to appear in John Garden's book **Nicholas Morant's Canadian Pacific**. This would be a large tome of photos that might possibly be the best book on railways ever conceived. Garden was a CP locomotive engineer out of Revelstoke and became acquainted with Morant through his exploits taking photos on the CP mainline. It has seen multiple printings and was an international hit in the 1990s.

Both Crump and Morant would be invested into the Order of Canada. Buck Crump would eventually go on in the 1960s helping rebrand Canadian Pacific into branches such as CP Rail, CP Air and CP Ships. He would become an honoured member of Canadian business called as a Companion of the Order of Canada in 1971. Morant would become a Member of the Order for his photography in 1990.

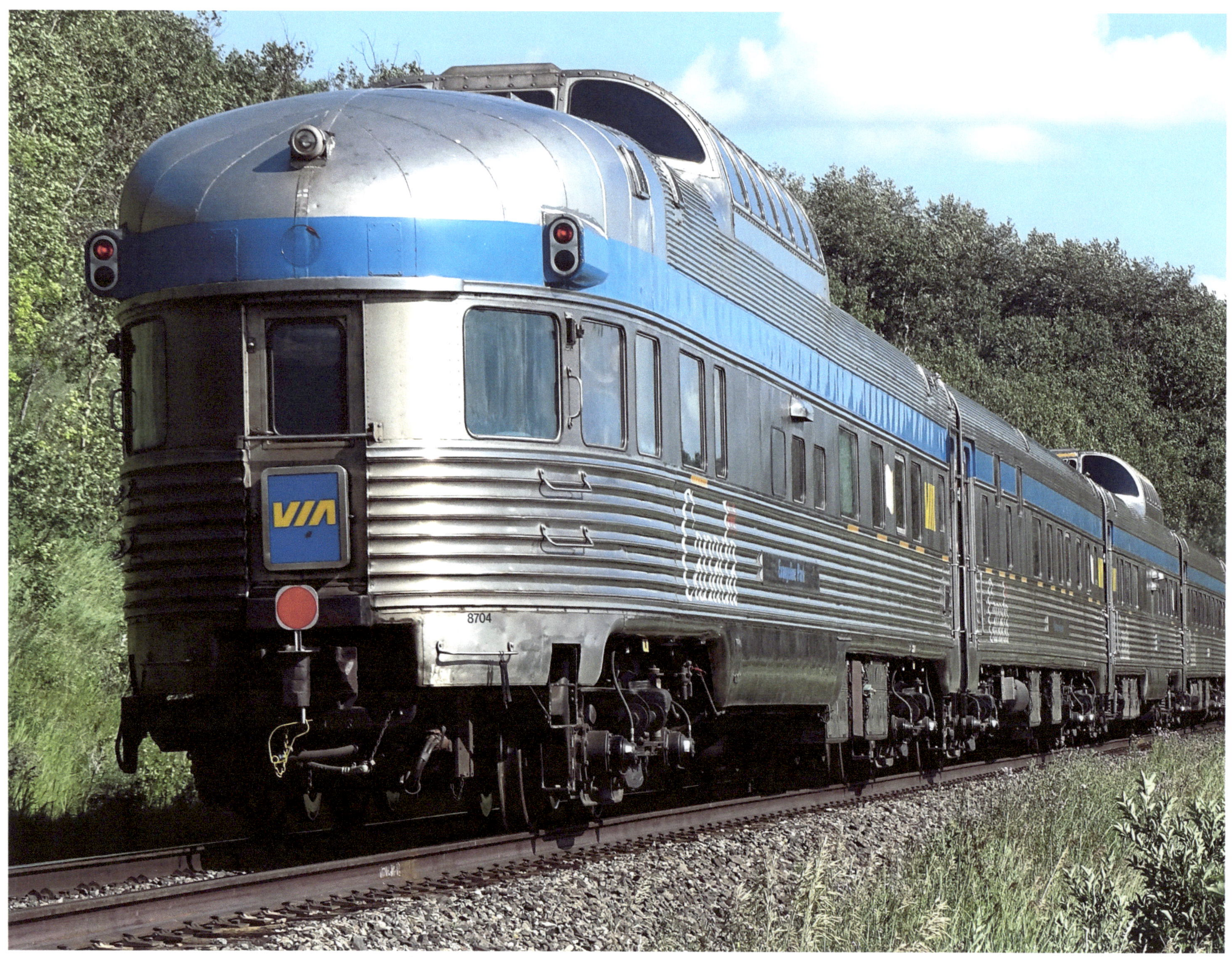
VIA
8704

The Creation of VIA Rail Canada

Buck Crump had ordered the stainless steel car fleet for Canadian Pacific Railway in 1953 on the assumption people would continue to ride the rails. There were changes to society coming in the late 1950s. Air travel was starting to become a choice for intercity travel and governments were putting money into road systems across North America. Soon the privacy and convenience of the automobile would surpass the comfort of rail passenger service.

Crump was initially pleased with the purchase and the debut of the equipment on CP's flagship train The Canadian in 1955, the same year he would become president of the railway. The first full season of operation of The Canadian saw the train carry 27 million passengers across Canada. Some dubbed the train "Buck's Beauty" in honour of Crump. A trip across Canada took only three nights and Crump saw personally as president that the train maintained its schedule.

Canadians were drawn to the tourist centers of Banff and Lake Louise in Alberta. At the time a train ride out of Toronto was viewed by many in southern Ontario as a blue collar dream holiday. Families saved for the day they could take The Canadian out west to the Rocky Mountains. However, competition from the airlines and automobile would eat into The Canadian's revenue. Entering the 1960s the train lost a quarter of its ridership.

The rise of the automobile affected rail service greatly. CP began petitioning to end service on a number of passenger runs in the late 1950s and early 1960s. By the mid-1960s The Canadian was being viewed as a detriment to the company's balance sheet. By this time Crump had realized that the purchase of the stainless steel fleet was a mistake in his opinion. A decision he would later say he would like to take back. Crump had told one reporter during this period that if The Canadian was full to capacity on every trip it would still not meet its operating costs.

This statement reflected the state of passenger rail service in North America at the time. CP's primary competitor Canadian National Railway tried to stem the tide of declining market share in the late 1960s. CN revitalized its fleet with second hand equipment from the United States and incorporated its Red, White and Blue fare system offering specific payment schedules for certain days of the week. CN would see an increase in ridership that would be helped somewhat by the World Exposition, Expo 67, being held in Montreal, Quebec and the increased tourism that came with it.

However, in the 1970s the losses on passenger services were taking their toll. CN, like CP, was eventually looking to get out of the passenger market and become a freight only operation.

VIA was created in 1976 under CN to market its passenger services. A garish blue and yellow paint scheme was unveiled for the passenger car and locomotive fleet. A timetable was released that advertised both CN and CP passenger schedules. The VIA name was bilingual and the logo is an ambigram that was designed by studio ARC Montreal's Gerhard Ade and Michael Williams. CN logos also adorned VIA's equipment at the time.

CP continued to operate the stainless steel train The Canadian. By this time CP was cutting service wherever it could to save money. Short winter time consists of a handful of cars were becoming normal for the train by the mid-1970s. CP's opportunity to rid itself of the train and other services such as the fast Rail Diesel Car (RDC) run between Calgary and Edmonton, Alberta came in 1978. This was following the creation of VIA as a separate government agency to oversee national passenger service.

VIA Rail Canada was formed by order of the Privy Council and signed into law by Prime Minister Pierre Trudeau in 1977. One thing that would hamper the government agency was the fact it was created by order of the Privy Council. Had it been created by an Act of Parliament the organization could raise money from outside investors and international money markets. As a result VIA was at the whim of the Canadian government's annual budget which would hold back this Crown Corporation.

The 1977 creation of VIA as a government agency would see CN and CP's passenger operations integrated. CN's fleet of cars were smooth side steel passenger cars painted by VIA in their blue corporate paint scheme and would be named the "Blue Fleet". CP's fleet were primarily the 1950s Budd built stainless steel cars. The red letterboard bands it wore as CP Rail equipment would quickly be changed to VIA blue. Eventually the two car fleets would be intermixed by 1980 and CP's The Canadian service would have the "The" dropped by VIA becoming simply "Canadian".

There was hope VIA could stop the erosion of Canada's rail passenger network. There was some initial confusion, train riders who had grown accustom to using a CN or CP train did not take to the VIA branding. Many assumed they were on a CN train at a CN station as they always had been. This would eventually change over the years as the VIA name became more accepted.

Being at the mercy of the federal government's budgets would not be kind to VIA. Cuts in 1981 by Transport Minister Jean-Luc Pepin would see a 40% reduction in train services with many runs ended. Later the Brian Mulroney government would reinstate some of these services in the mid-1980s but devastating cuts would come under his government in 1989. VIA was forced to scratch 55% of its services. The Canadian service would be cancelled by VIA and end service to most communities along the CP mainline in January 1990. Small and large centers ranging from places such as Kenora, Ontario to Calgary, Alberta would lose their only intercity passenger service. The Canadian name would then be used on the CN transcontinental mainline route replacing the Super Continental that had also been cut.

It would be the end of an era bemoaned by proud Canadian patriots across the country. The Canadian had been considered a national treasure which VIA continued to operate despite the drastic cuts. The stainless steel equipment would carry on operating with VIA. In their fifth decade of service by the 1990s, they were to become the backbone of VIA's fleet.

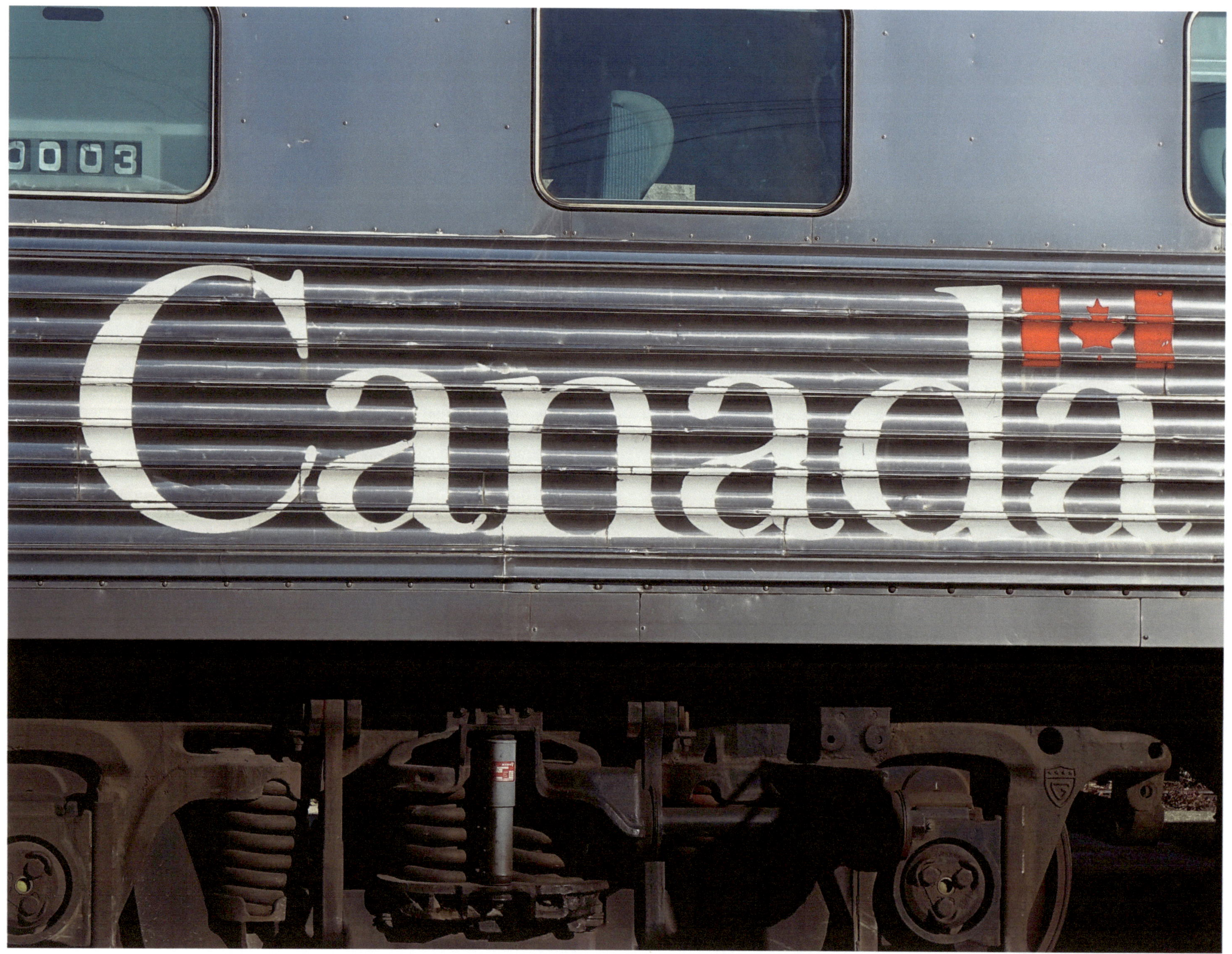

0003
Canada

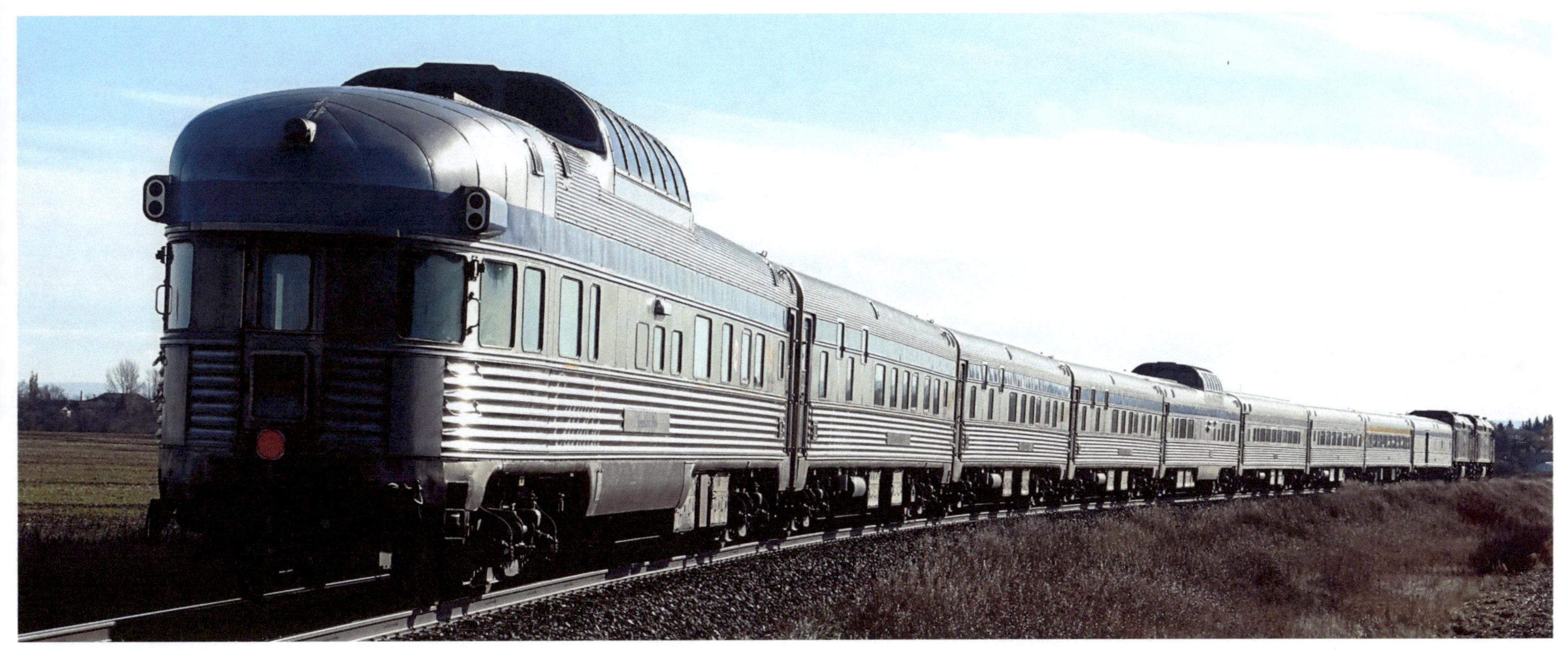

Initially the stainless steel cars were steam heated. Pipes ran through the cars and hoses connected them between couplings. A steam generator in the locomotives pulling the train or a specially built steam generator car provided the heat.

Winter operations caused problems for this concept. Steam heat leaked from the hose connections between cars and operational difficulties resulted with the build up of ice. It was proven that this was not a reliable system but had been the accepted practice for North American railroads dating back to the era when steam locomotives pulled the trains.

VIA experimented with an Amtrak train set in the mid-1980s in Western Canada to test out the General Motors F40 diesel locomotive and Superliner double deck coaches that were electric heated. VIA officials were impressed with the concept but did not order the Superliner cars. They did order the F40 with HEP (Head End Power) to provide electricity and decided instead to rebuild its existing coach fleet announcing the HEP rebuild program in 1987. These cars would accompany the order for new locomotives.

However, the VIA car rebuild took some time to materialize. VIA ran the F40PH-2D's it ordered with older GM and Montreal Locomotive Works power that could provide steam heat to the existing cars. This meant the F40 would take the lead on trains as it did not have the through steam heat connections.

The former CP Budd cars were found to be in great shape after having provided over 30 years of service. VIA decided to use the stainless steel cars as the basis for its HEP program and they would form the backbone of the VIA fleet. During 1991 these rebuilt cars began entering service with VIA paired with the 6400 series F40 locomotives as intended. These cars eventually became known as HEP1 cars.

The stainless steel equipment can be found throughout the VIA system. VIA utilizes this equipment on a regular basis in Western Canada on the Canadian operating between Toronto and Vancouver; the "Skeena" between Jasper, Alberta and Prince Rupert, British Columbia and the Churchill service from Winnipeg to Churchill, Manitoba. VIA also uses the equipment on some trains in the Windsor - Quebec City Corridor and on northern Quebec services.

The Montreal to Halifax, Nova Scotia "Ocean" service does see stainless steel equipment. In recent years Renaissance cars that were purchased from England in 2000 served the train but Park dome-observation cars were also assigned. There is also a unique operation using Budd built Rail Diesel Cars (RDC) in north-central Ontario. These cars look very much like a regular Budd built stainless steel coach and carry diesel prime movers making it a self-propelled car. They operate on the CP mainline between Sudbury and White River, Ontario providing remote service to people along the line.

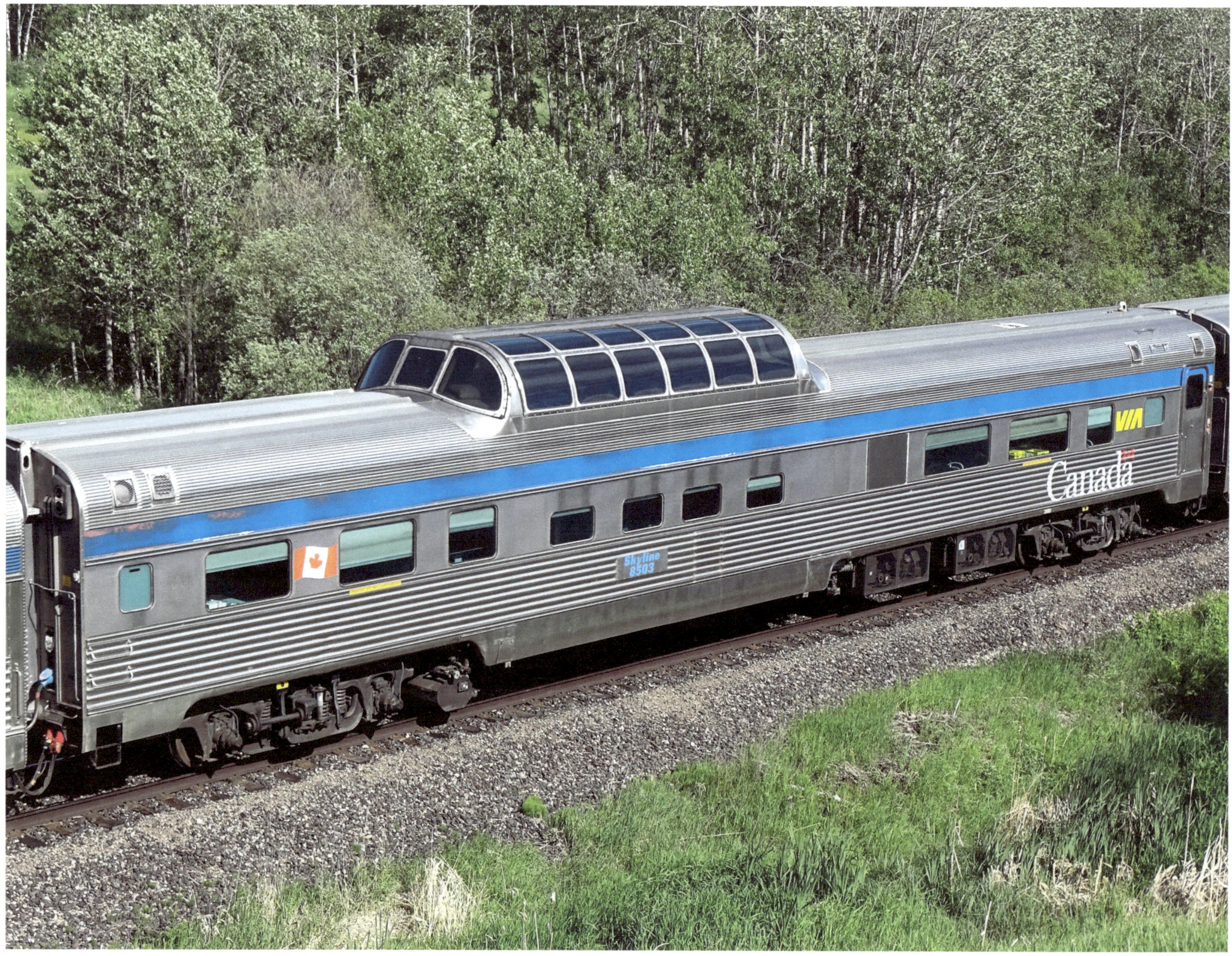
VIA
Canada
Skyline
8503

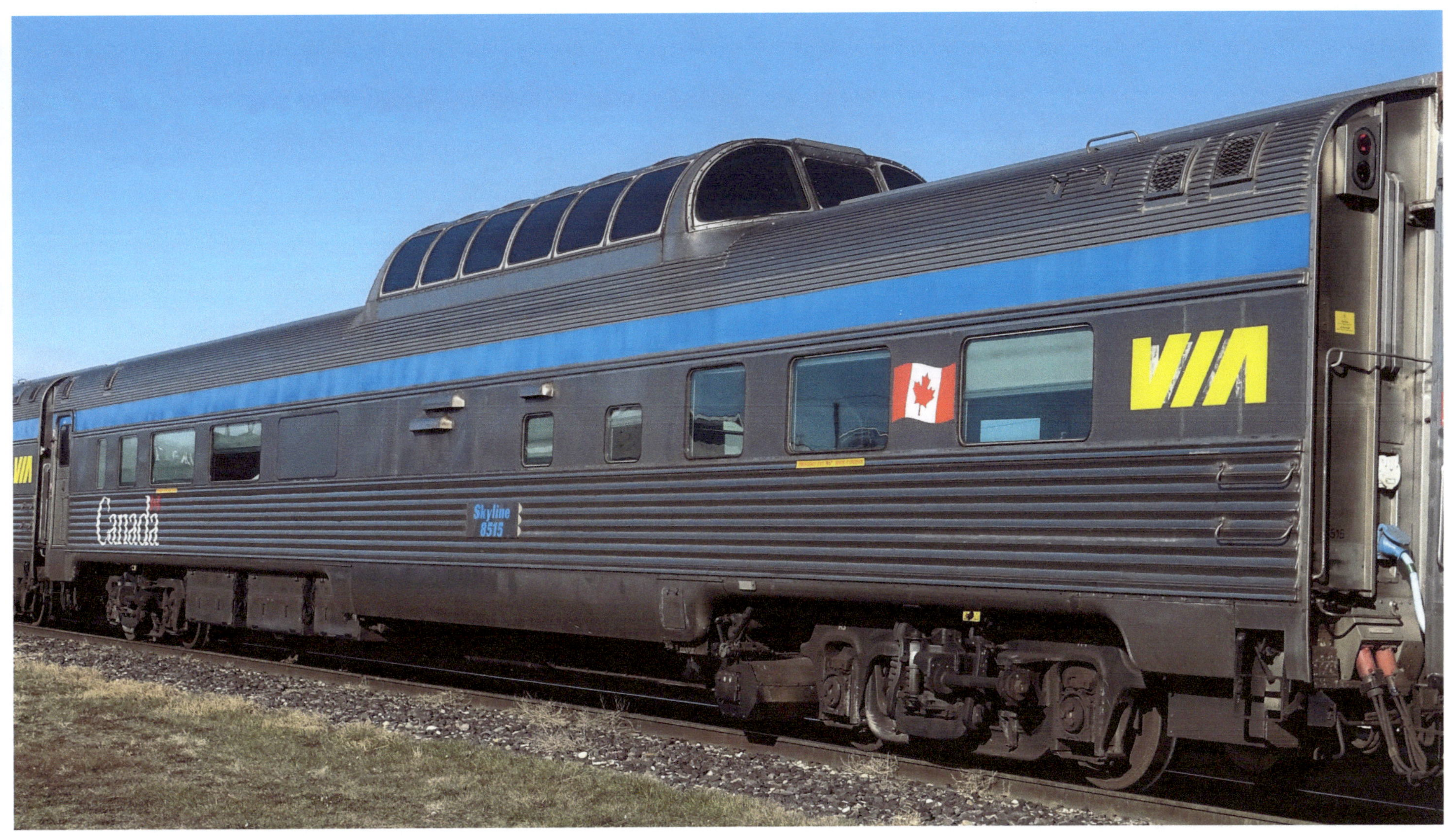

The primary feature thought of with the streamlined cars is the dome car. VIA operates the Skyline dome mid-train and the Park dome-observation car at the end of some consists.

18 Skyline dome cars were ordered in the original CP order for The Canadian in the 1950s. These cars featured the dome area on the upper level and a separate seating area and lounge area in the lower level when built. VIA reorganized this in 1983 placing a dining area in the same space. Through rebuilds the cars were also turned around from their original configuration with the dome car's shorter end facing forward during operation. Seating was turned around to accommodate this.

The Skyline name was derived from the Skyline Trail Hikers of the Canadian Rockies. It was created by John Gibbon who was in charge of publicity for the Canadian Pacific Railway. Gibbon thought up the idea to give tourists in the Banff, Alberta area something to do during their stay. It was primarily an activity including horseback riding in its infancy. During 1933 the Skyline name was adopted by Gibbon and it involved hiking between encampments and lodges.

The cars were numbered in the 500 series by CP and would be renumbered in the 8500 series when they emerged from VIA Rail's HEP program in the 1990s. They have a capacity of 48 people.

The original CP Skyline cars featured murals in the lounge area, some painted by French artist Pierre Bourdelle. Bourdelle's father Emile-Antoine was an assistant to famous French sculptor Auguste Rodin. As the cars went through refurbishment over the years the murals were removed.

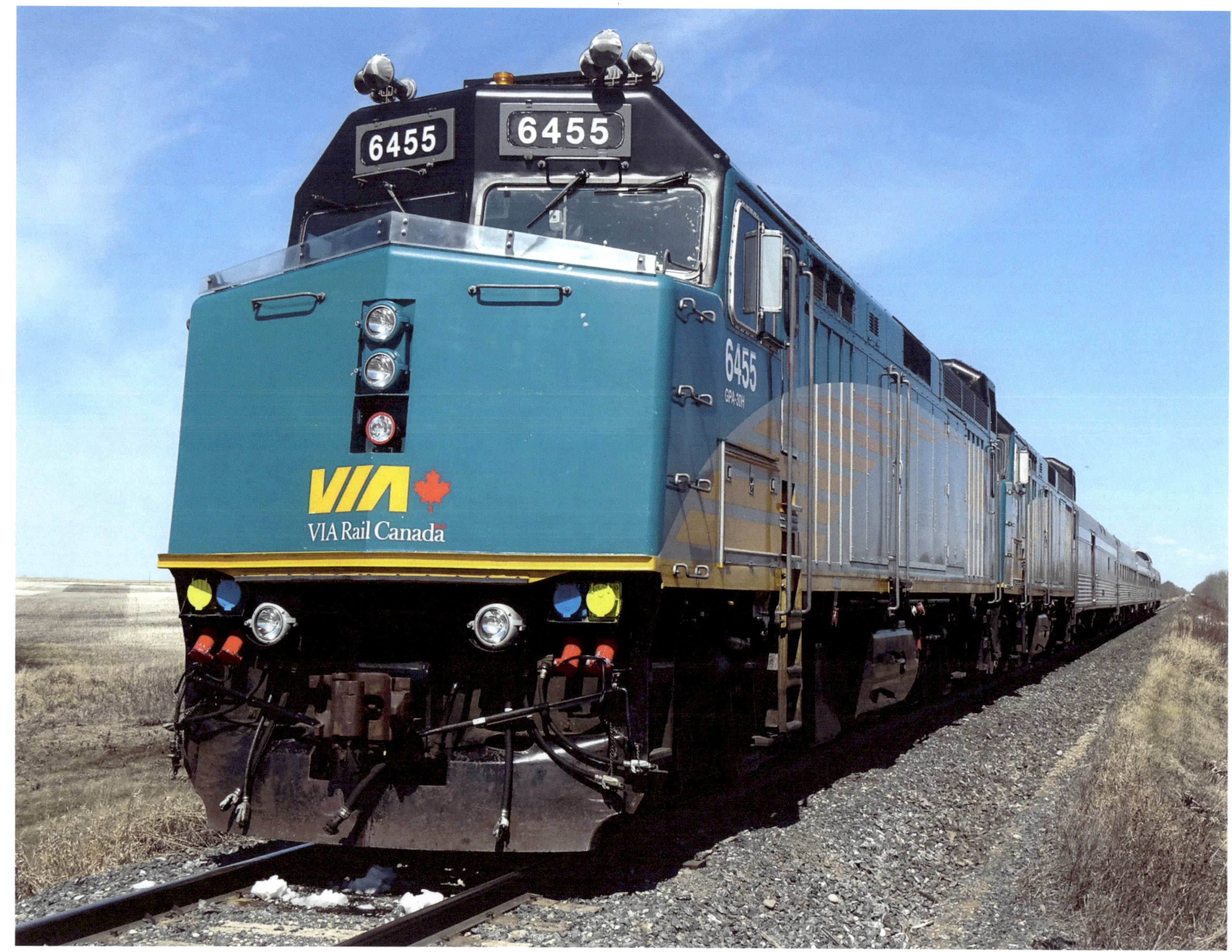
6455
6455
6455
GPA-30H
VIA
VIA Rail Canada

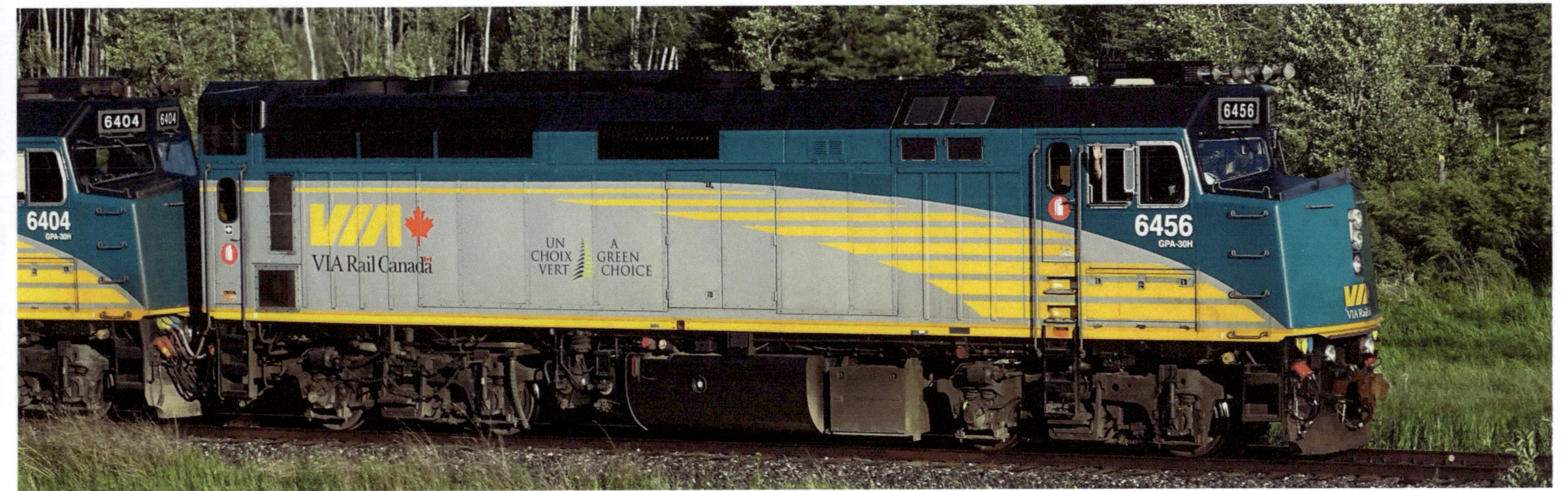

The locomotive workhorse for VIA Rail is the F40PH-2D, the 6400 series. The first examples arrived on the roster in late 1986. The General Motors F40 had been the prime choice for a passenger locomotive by US railroads and an Amtrak version was tested by VIA on the Panorama passenger run in Western Canada. VIA was impressed with the engine's performance and went to General Motors Diesel Division in London, Ontario to design a version for Canadian operating conditions.

The F40PH-2D featured a 3000 horsepower 16 cylinder EMD 645E3C engine that could generate up to 3300 horsepower if required. It is equipped with a full width car body that protected operators in winter conditions.

The F40 featured HEP (Head End Power), a feature that allowed the locomotive to provide electricity for heat to the train cars. One drawback of the HEP feature was that it required the locomotive to idle at high revs when stopped to run the generator that provided the electricity. The HEP generator was driven off the main engine, this caused lower horsepower to be generated by the prime mover when the HEP system was engaged.

VIA began using the units in the Windsor - Quebec City Corridor initially and then by the summer of 1987 they could be found on the premier VIA train the Canadian. Usually they were paired with much older General Motors F9B locomotives that could provide steam heat to the coaches.

The author remembers well meeting a designer from GM at Benmiller near Goderich, Ontario in the 1980s. They were justifiably proud of the work being done at the London plant and the F40PH-2D was one of the locomotives being manufactured then.

While train enthusiasts referred to the unit as the F40PH-2D, which was the General Motors designation for the unit, VIA and its operating crews called it the GPA30. This was a CN inspired motive power designation.

The G stood for General Motors, the P for passenger, A was for an engine capable of leading or A-unit. The 30 stood for 3000 horsepower.

As part of the technical requirements for the diesel, the unit was fit with a desktop control stand, something that was becoming standard on CN delivered engines. The GM name for the unit had caused speculation that the "D" designation in the F40PH-2D noted that the unit had desktop controls. This has been somewhat controversial in recent years. Suggestions have been made that the D may actually stand for Diesel Division, the Canadian branch of GM in London that fully designed and built the unit for VIA.

VIA would receive 59 of these 6400 series units between 1986 and 1989. They would replace older General Motors and Montreal Locomotive Works diesels and would eventually become the main locomotive in the VIA fleet. Originally delivered in a yellow, grey and blue scheme these engines could be found throughout the VIA system.

During the early 2000s VIA purchased 21 General Electric locomotives to provide service on the Eastern Corridor but they never strayed out of that assignment. As a result the 6400s became the primary power for regional services and the transcontinental Canadian.

VIA decided to rebuild the units in 2007 after having a test unit from the series refurbished in 2006. It announced a new program to revitalize the F40 fleet and CAD Railway Industries in Lachine, Quebec received the contract. This would see the locomotives equipped with a separate HEP generator that would allow for fuel conservation on the units. 6402 would be the first unit released in 2009 and featured a new paint scheme, "A Green Choice". By 2012 the entire roster of 6400 series units were rebuilt and back in service. The refurbishment would allow the F40 to continue operating for up to another 20 years.

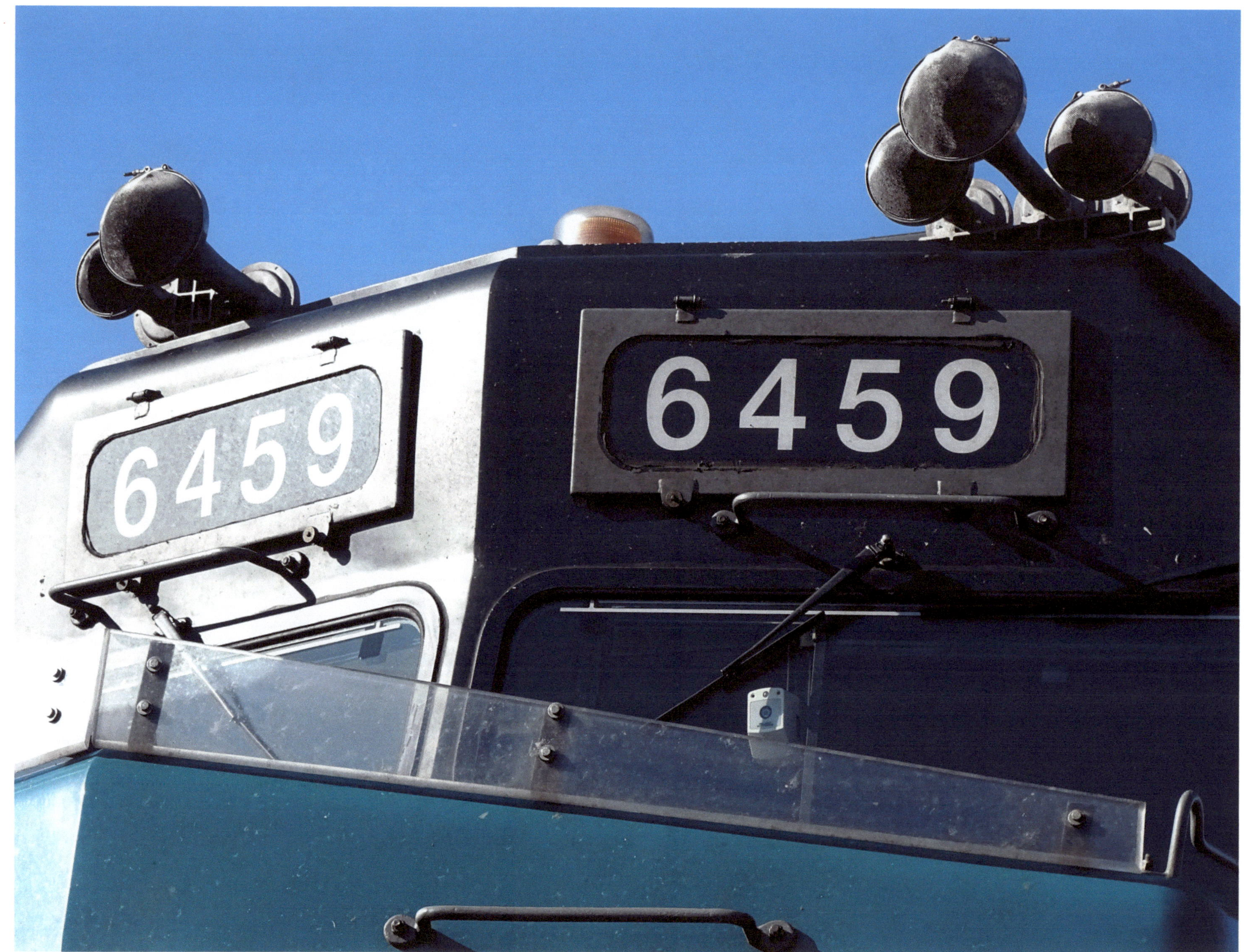

6459
6459

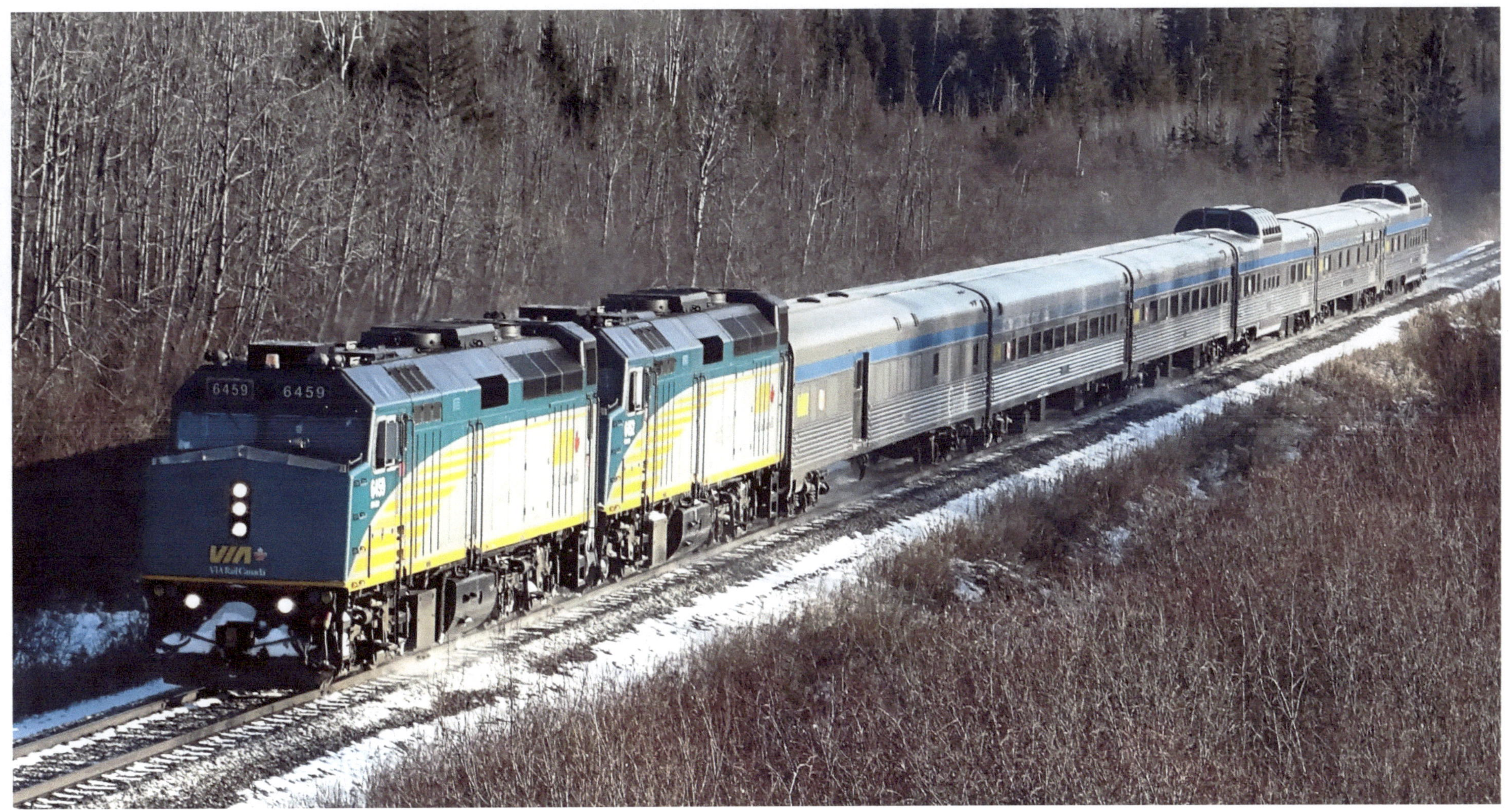

VIA engine 6459 is shown on these pages as it has become somewhat of a celebrity on the VIA Rail roster. 6459 was originally numbered 6403 and as such would gain fame as the lead locomotive on the Canadian passenger train image used on the Canadian $10 bill starting in 2013.

6403 was also noted for being in a scheme representing the Canadian Broadcasting Corporation on its 50th anniversary in 2002. It would pull a consist of stainless steel baggage cars containing displays of CBC historical items across Canada. 6403 would undergo rebuilding at CAD Industries in Lachine, Quebec before being immortalized on the reverse of the $10 currency.

VIA decided to renumber the 6403 to 6459 in the event there was some unforeseen event such as an accident that would tarnish the reputation of the railway or the Canadian currency. As a result the 6403 number was retired from service. The $10 note depicted the Canadian train running through a "S" curve in the Rocky Mountains. The backdrop would be a depiction of the Canadian Rockies standing tall. It was a composite image of the various mountains in Jasper National Park along VIA's Canadian route.

In the photo on the left 6459 shows off the emergency horns installed during rebuilding by CAD Railway Industries. These are K5CA-LS horns that were a new standard being mandated by Transport Canada. The horns can play a loud deep sound in "emergency" mode with five chimes. The emergency mode is typically used to warn animals or people close to the tracks as the train approaches. The rebuilt VIA units still carry the regular K3L three chime horn that was originally delivered on the F40.

Above 6459 leads the Churchill train out of the Shell River Valley in western Manitoba on a cold November day. This service is based out of VIA's Winnipeg Maintenance Centre.

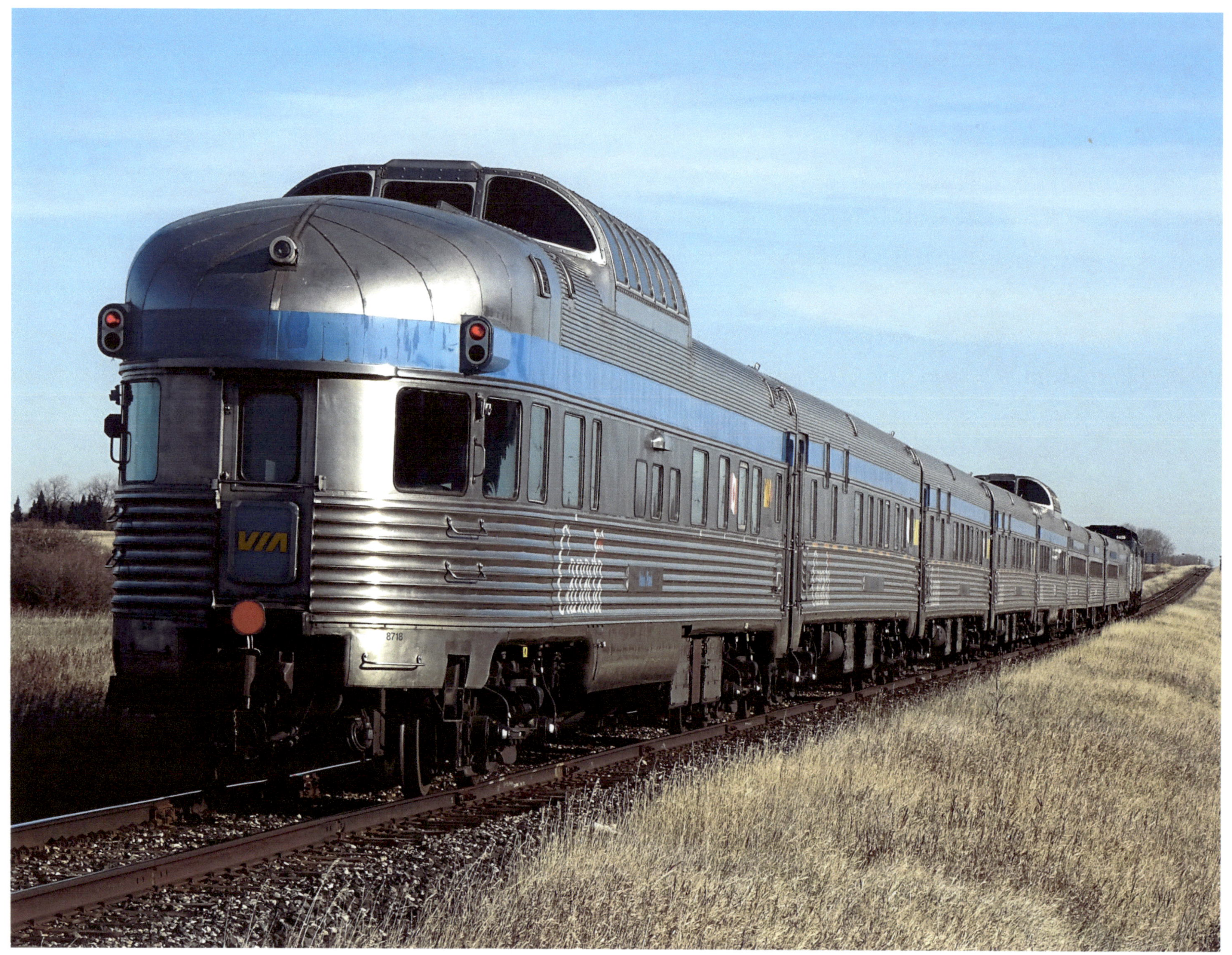

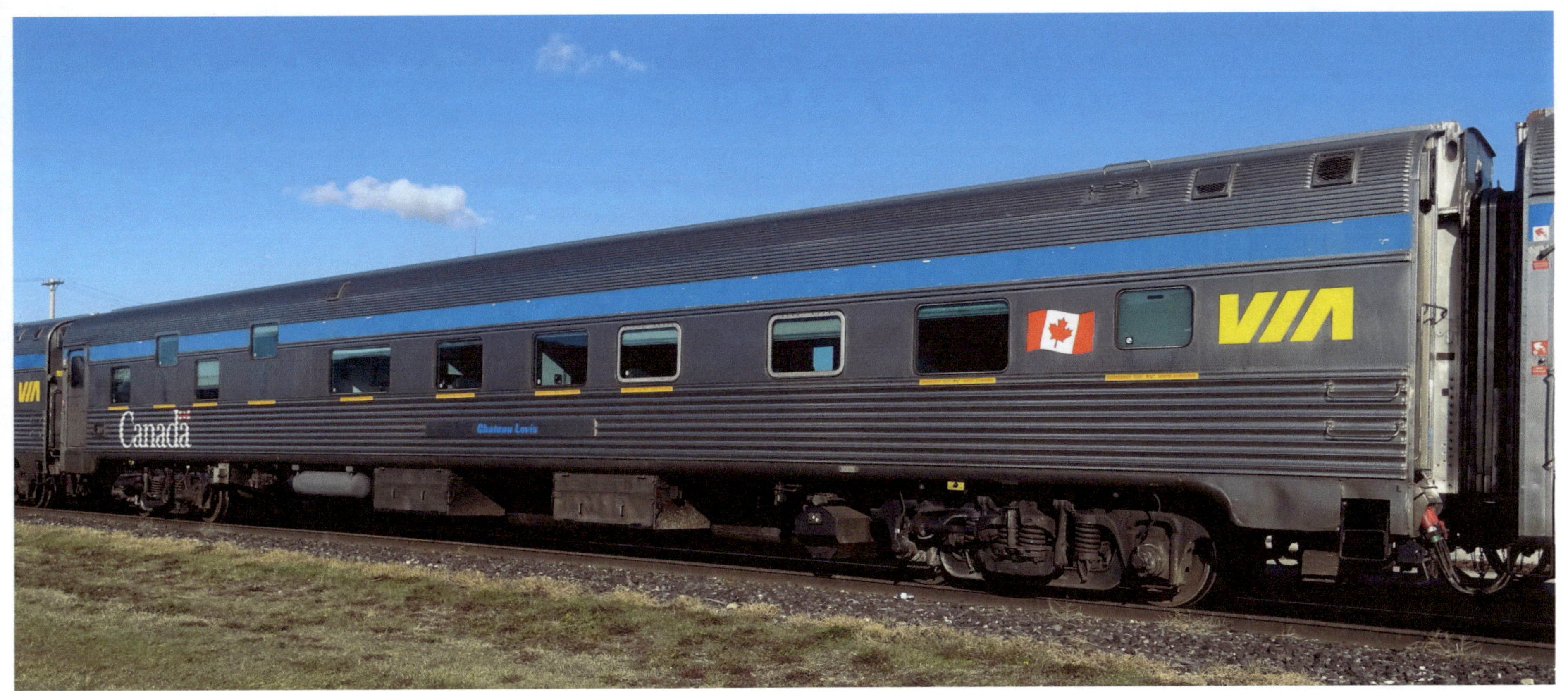

VIA also inherited from CP a number of sleeping cars. These were divided into two car types, the Chateau sleeper and the Manor sleeper. The Chateau cars were noted for their unusual staggered window arrangement at the end of the car. This was to provide a view for the upper and lower duplex roomettes the car featured. Above is Chateau Levis.

The Chateau cars were named after French figures of history. The Manor cars, which see service on the Canadian, were named after prominent English historical individuals. The Manor series cars featured more bedrooms than roomettes while the Chateau series were the opposite.

VIA refurbished these cars under its HEP program in the 1990s and they are considered HEP1 cars. VIA announced a new round of funding for rebuilding cars in 2009, overhauling the Manor sleepers first as part of the announcement.

While Buck Crump would view his purchase of the stainless steel cars in the 1950s as a mistake, fate would be kind to him and the cars turned out to be technologically designed marvels. The stainless steel design held up well in the Canadian winters and held up to corrosion.

When purchasing the cars Crump used his education at Purdue University as a mechanical engineer to make his decisions. He was taken with the strong qualities that stainless steel possessed and was well acquainted with the manufacturing process.

Cold-worked austenitic stainless steel or CWASS is what the Budd cars CP ordered were made from. This steel contained elements of carbon, chromium, copper, manganese, nickel and silicon.

Edward Budd founded the Budd Company in 1912 in Philadelphia, Pennsylvania. Its original purpose was to make steel frames for automobiles and was one of the first manufacturers to use spot welding.

In 1930 Budd would visit Europe and learnt a great deal about stainless steel and the process to manufacture it. The ability for the Allegheny Steel Company to make high quality stainless steel and the Budd Company's experience in spot welding helped Edward Budd corner the market for passenger rail cars.

The Burlington Railroad looked at designing a passenger train using these materials. The Budd Company would build the Zephyr, released in 1934. Its design captured the imagination of the American public. The Zephyr was lightweight due to the use of stainless steel and could be powered by a diesel engine, it changed the face of railroading.

VIA Rail's stainless steel fleet continues to soldier on through the 2000s. It is well maintained and refurbishments have allowed it to be the workhorse of the passenger car fleet. Crump's initial decision paid off.

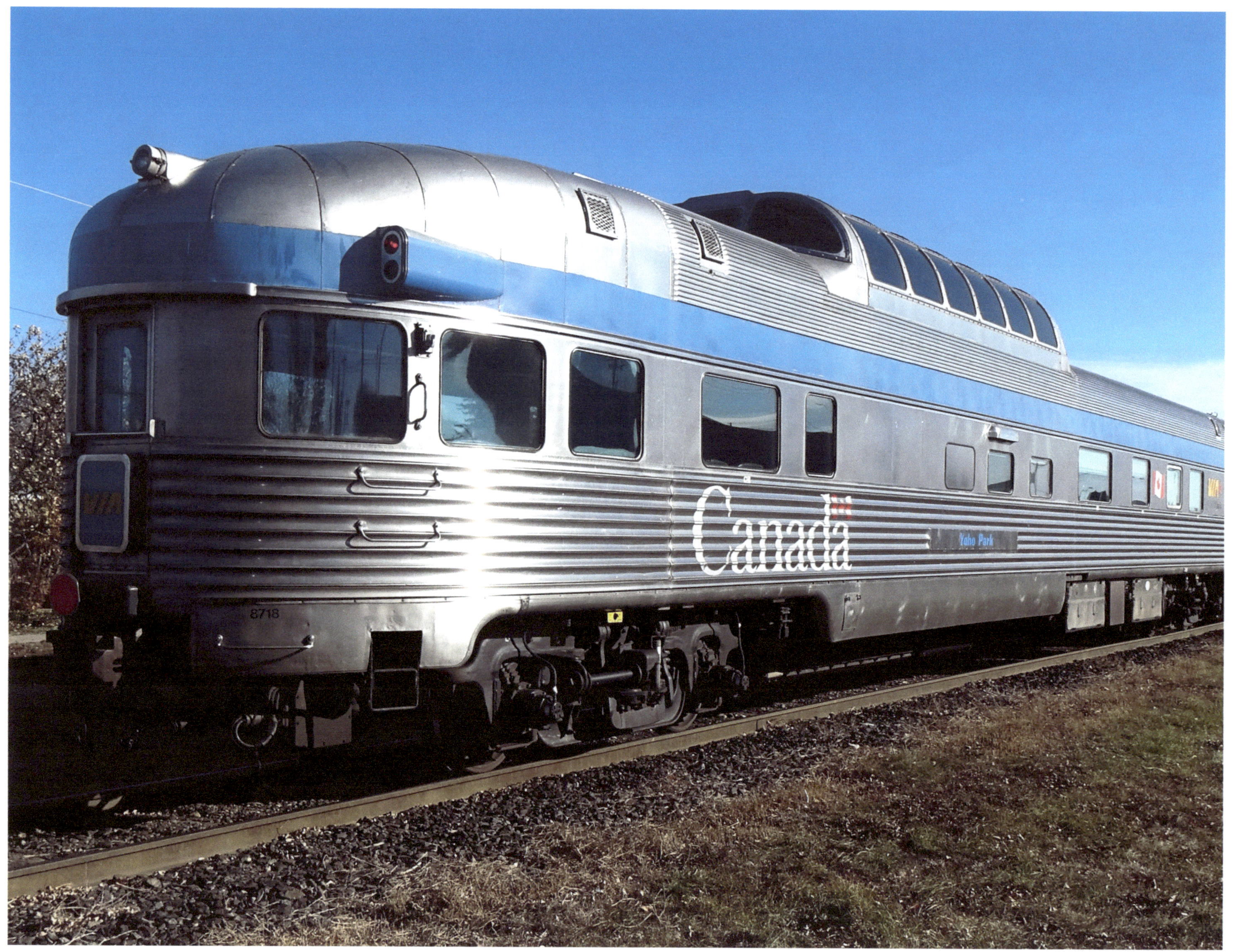

VIA
Canada
Yoho Park
8718

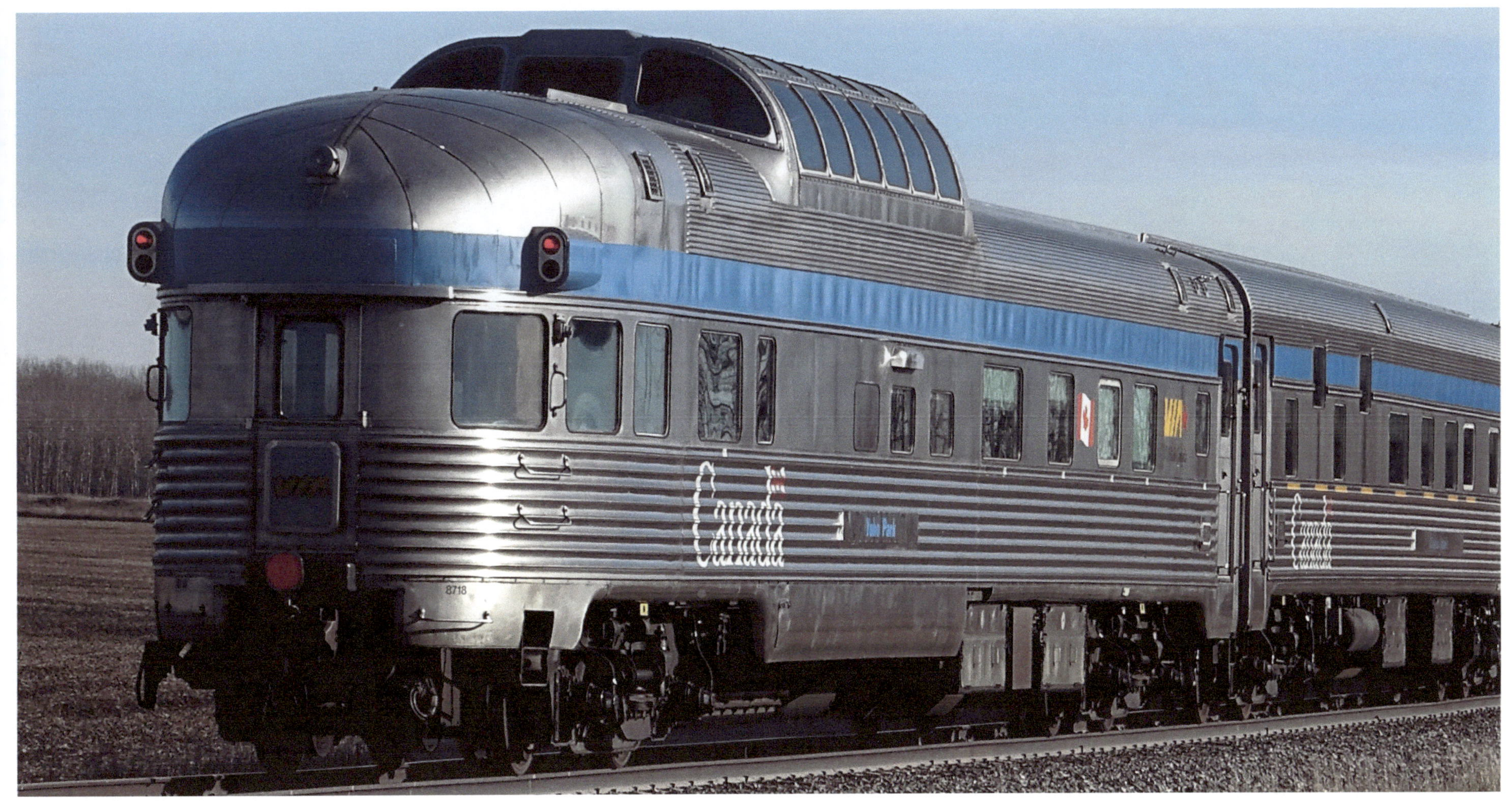

The star of the stainless steel fleet is the dome-observation Park car. These cars appear regularly on the Jasper to Prince Rupert Skeena train and the Canadian between Vancouver and Toronto. They have appeared on the Ocean service to Halifax and occasionally appear on the Churchill train service to northern Manitoba.

18 Park cars were purchased by Canadian Pacific in its order for equipment for The Canadian in the mid-1950s. The cars were primarily named after Canadian provincial and national parks closely served by the CPR. Yoho Park is seen in these two images.

The cars featured a number of decorative motifs, the most noted being murals painted by members of the Royal Canadian Academy of Arts. CP had contacted the academy and a number of painters were chosen for the work.

Each car had a mural corresponding to the park it was named after.

Three Group of Seven artists participated, A.J. Casson with a mural of Algonquin Park and A.Y. Jackson of Kokanee Park. Edwin Holgate decorated the car Tremblant Park. 18 artists painted the murals for the 18 CP cars. It was indicated that the artists received over $1000 for each mural commissioned which is valued at well over $10000 in today's currency. During the 1980s VIA removed the murals and displayed them publicly as the cars were refurbished. New murals were later installed.

Some Park cars have been rebuilt recently by 2015 for service on VIA's Canadian passenger train set. New larger sleeping cabins were added with larger windows to the Park cars and also a handful of Chateau class sleepers. The cars wear a dark grey letterboard band above the windows of the car to note that this is the Prestige Class part of the train, a service that comes at a premium price. The Prestige Class has added an air of sophistication to the Canadian train service from Toronto to Vancouver.

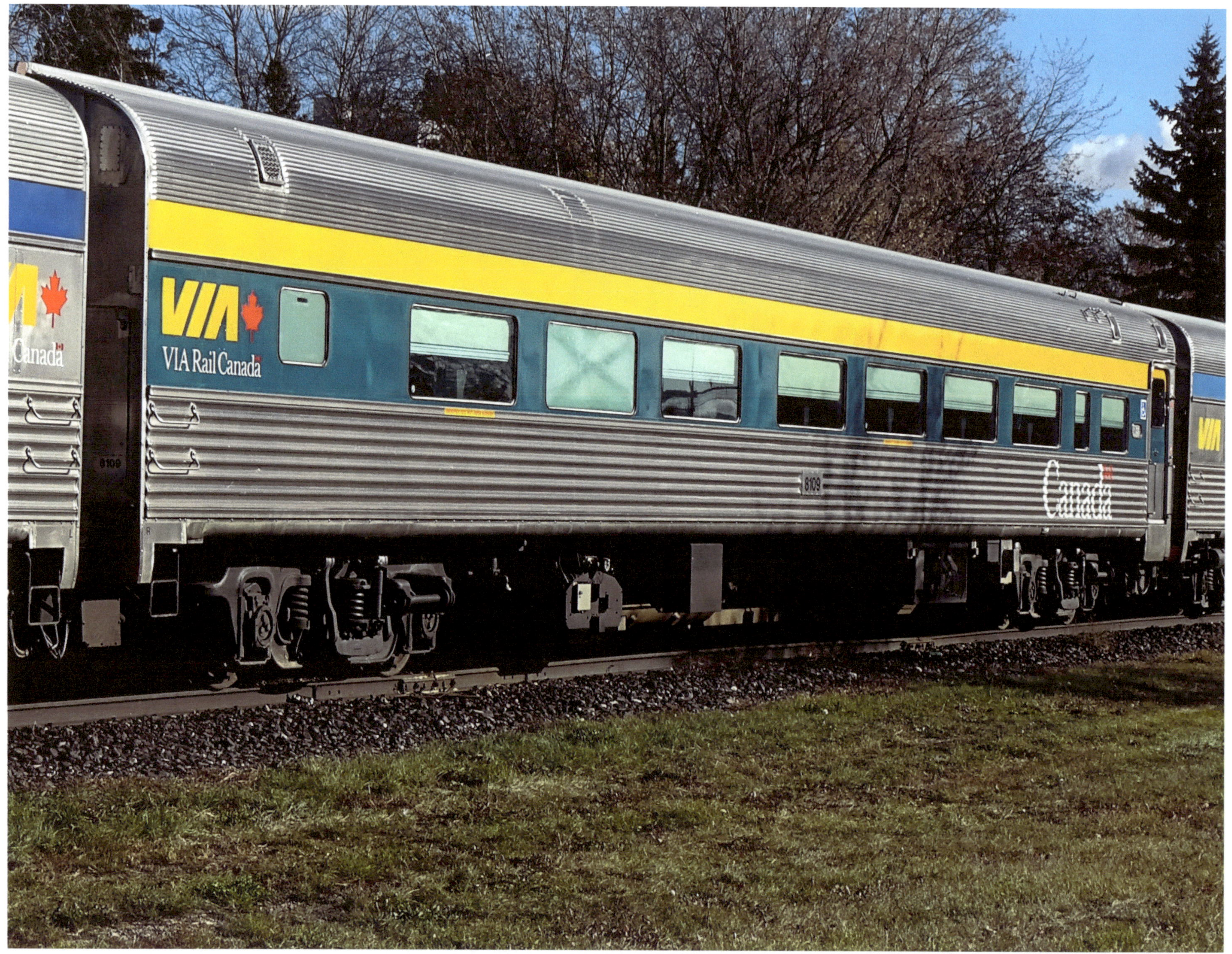

VIA
VIA Rail Canada
Canada
8109

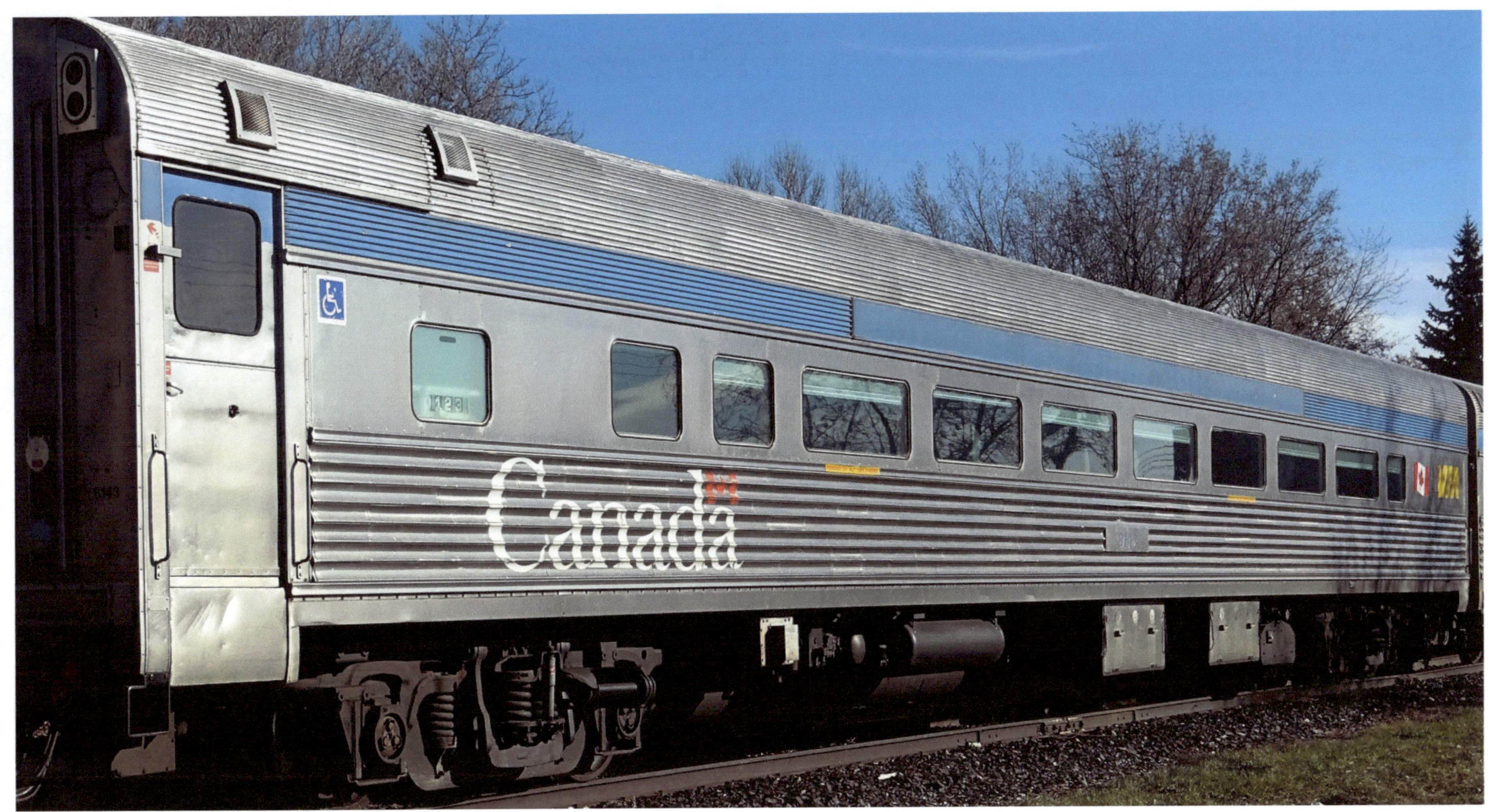

VIA Rail's coach fleet for economy class is a mix of Canadian Pacific cars delivered in the mid-1950s and a number of former American railroad cars purchased for the HEP (Head End Power) rebuild of the late 1980s and 1990s. Above VIA coach 8143 is shown. 8143 is one of the American cars picked up around 1990 and is one of the oldest cars to continue serving in the VIA fleet.

VIA 8143's history dates back prior to the United States entry in World War II. This car and others were part of a batch ordered by the Pennsylvania Railroad for a pool service with the Atlantic Coast Line Railroad in June 1941. The order was not completed until 1946 and this car would serve as PRR 4053. It was originally configured as a 54 seat coach. PRR 4053 would survive into the Penn Central era and the creation of Amtrak in the early 1970s. It would eventually be officially retired by Amtrak in 1981 and would be one of the American cars VIA would acquire

for rebuild with electric heat and power connections. The VIA rebuilding would see the car numbered 8143 and the capacity increased to 62 seats.

At left VIA 8109 is shown. 8109 was delivered with the original CP order in the 1950s for The Canadian train set. It was numbered 109 by CP and this number was used by VIA prior to rebuild into a HEP1 coach. The car featured 62 seats following rebuild with many that could be rotated so customers could face in the direction of travel if need be. A folding leg rest could be deployed to allow the passenger to rest their legs to sleep.

8109's appearance differs from the other stainless steel cars. The car was rebuilt during the spring of 2020 by CAD Industries in Montreal as part of VIA's program to revitalize the existing fleet. The car emerged with a yellow letterboard band and a teal blue hue through the window area. 8109 and others of this rebuild meet disability requirements as required by Canadian law.

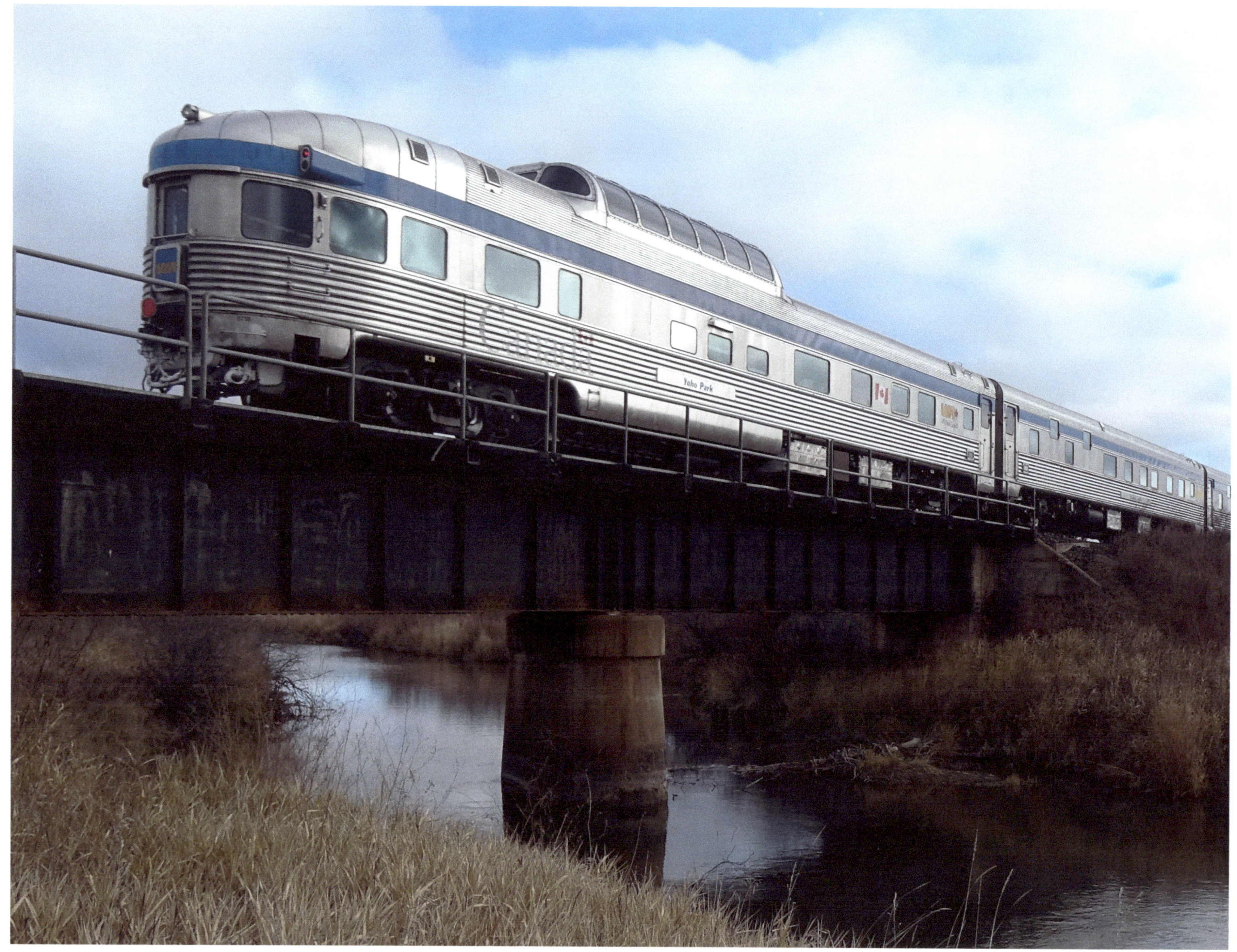

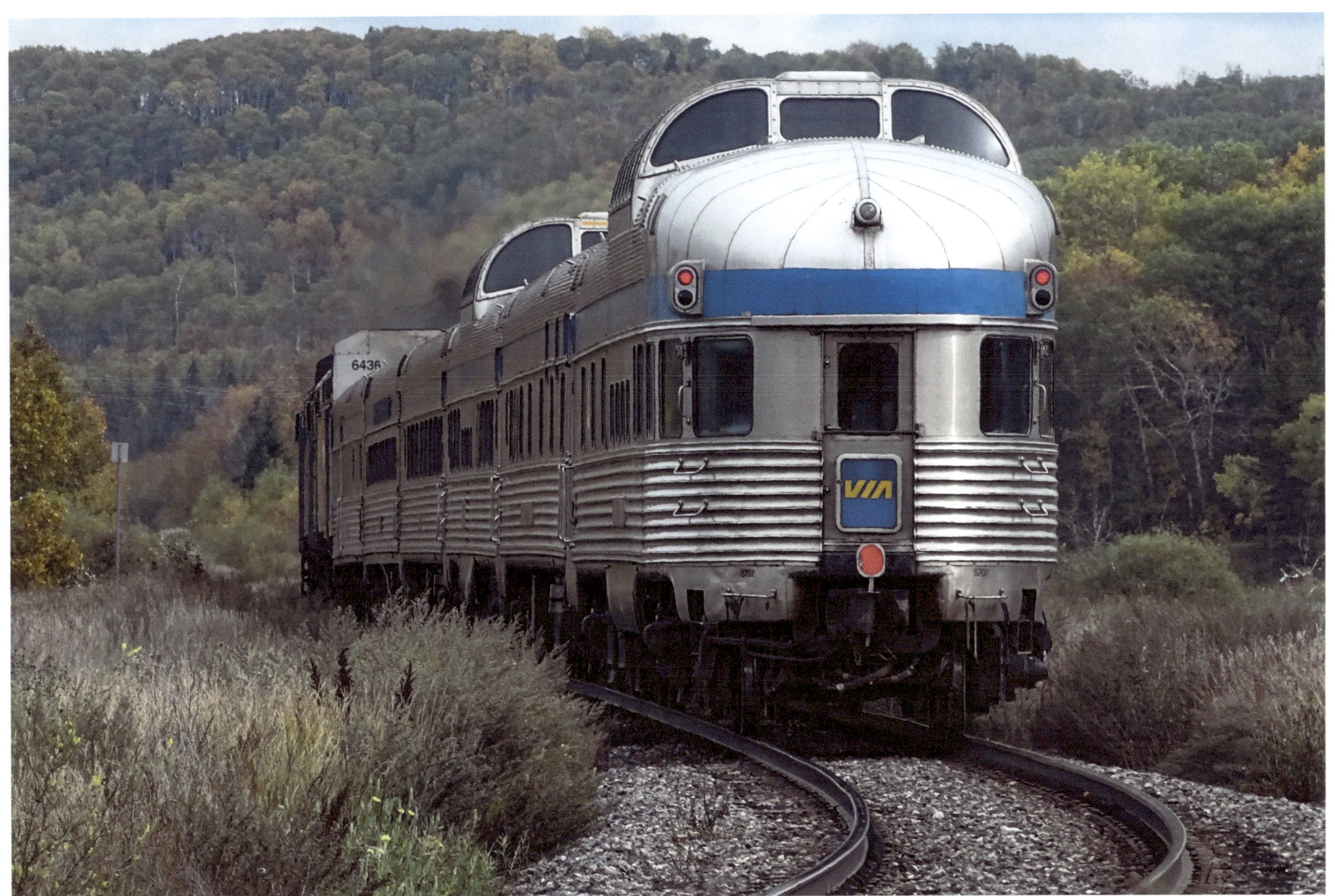

At left VIA Rail Canada train 692 is seen going over the Shell River at Shevlin in the western part of Manitoba. Above the train is seen dropping down through the scenic valley to the river crossing
The Shell River's origins date back thousands of years. The river was a tributary from the melting Keewatin Ice Flow that was part of the Laurentide Ice Sheet forming a deep valley. The resulting water flow is known as a misfit stream, noting that the river occupies a channel that does not complement its size. The Shell currently flows out of the Duck Mountains.
A small community still exists at Shevlin, home to a handful of houses. It is in the middle of gradients on Canadian National Railway's Togo Subdivision. This line is considered by many railroaders to be one of the more scenic routes in Western Canada.

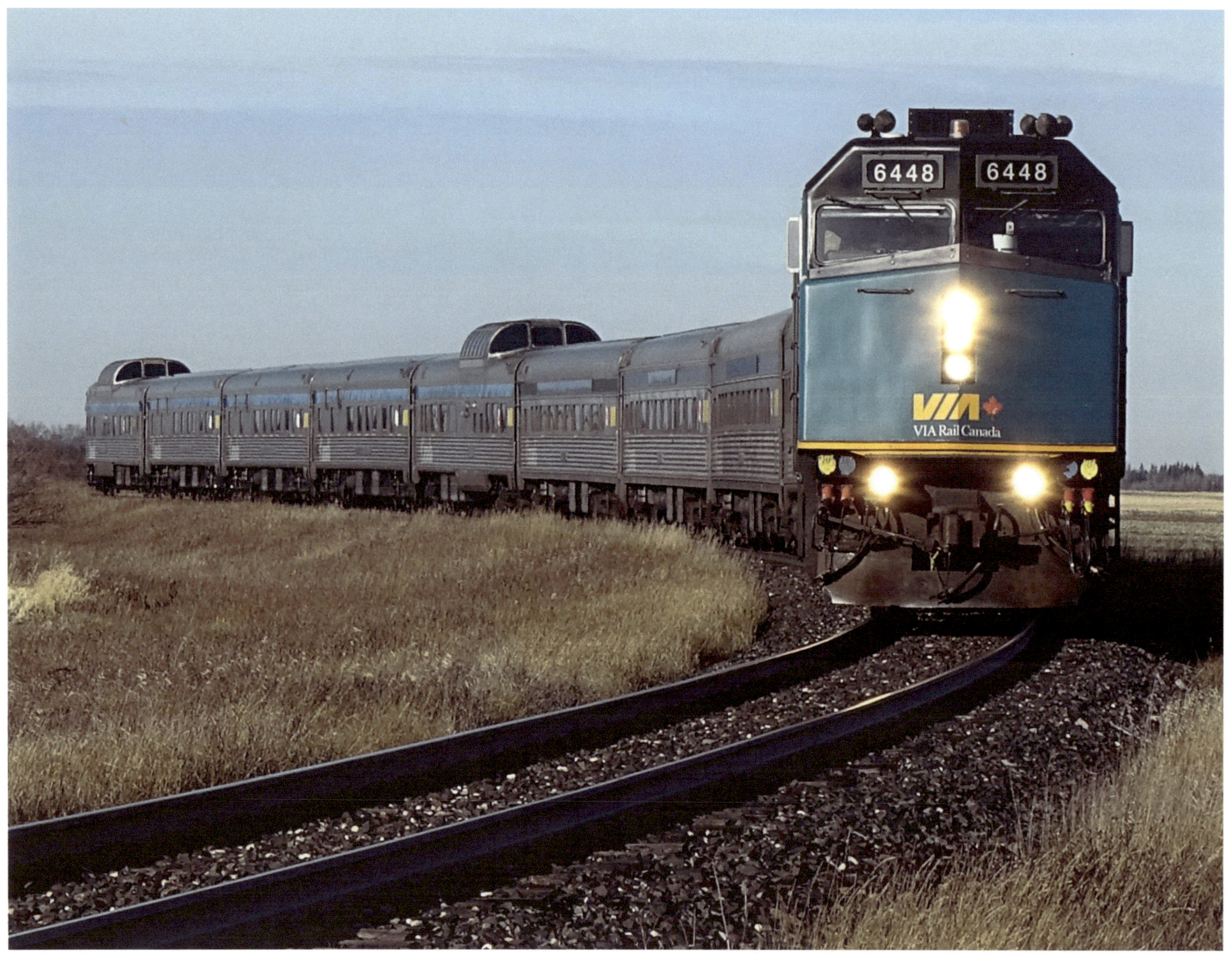

6448
6448
VIA
VIA Rail Canada

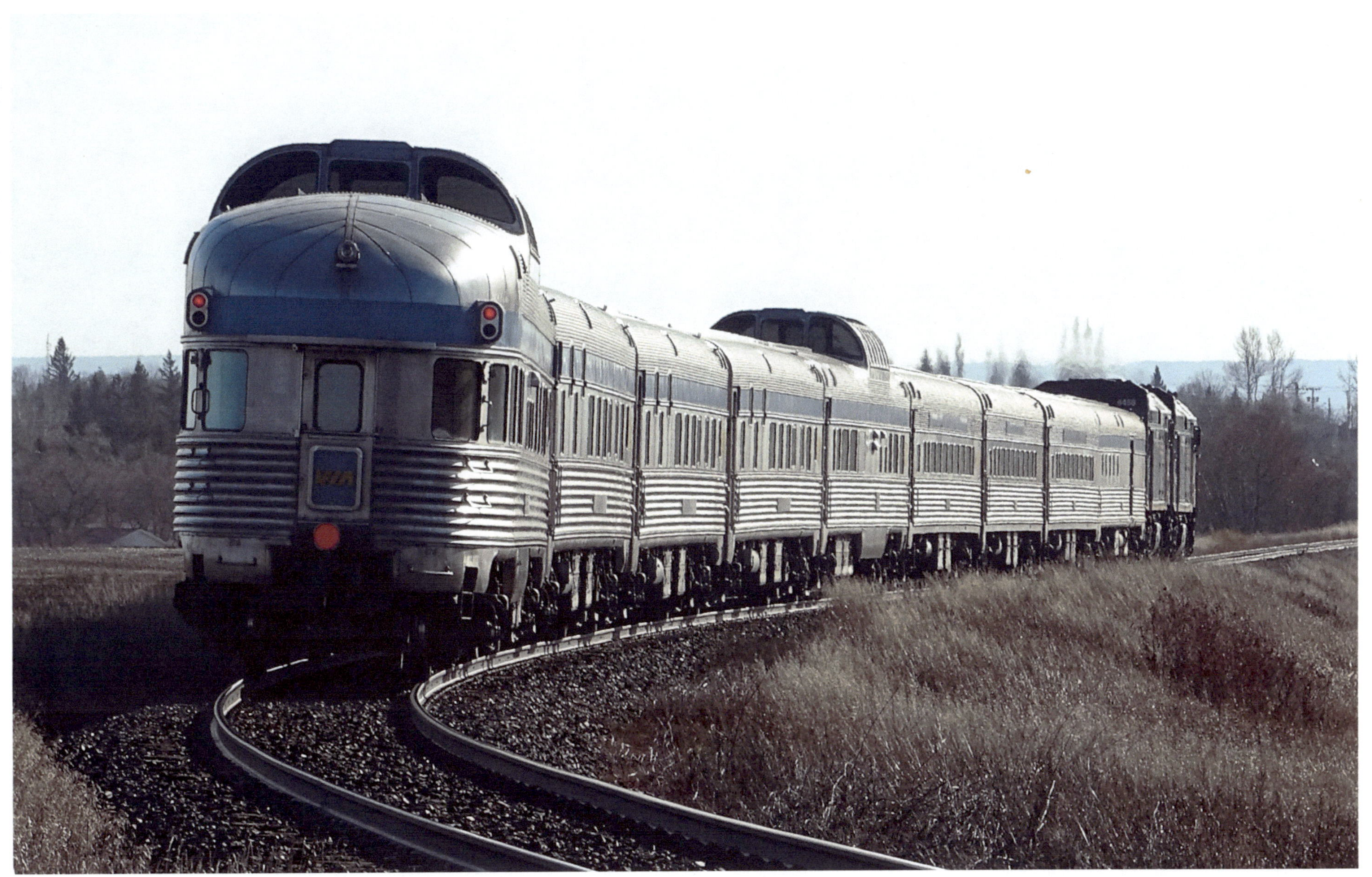

VIA 692, the Churchill train, is seen approaching the town of Grandview, Manitoba. Grandview is nestled in between Riding Mountain National Park to the south and Duck Mountain Provincial Park to the north. It is a scenic area and is home to many forms of wildlife. Primarily a grain farming region, logging takes place north of the area.

Grandview was founded following the arrival of the Canadian Northern Railway and became the location of a large wooden and steel trestle bridge over the Valley River. The community was incorporated in 1906.

Visible above in the distance is Riding Mountain National Park. It was officially declared a national park during 1933. The park is centered around beautiful Clear Lake and it was created to protect ecosystems such as grasslands and boreal forests.

VIA train 692 and northward counterpart 693 run between Winnipeg and Churchill, Manitoba. This service draws tourists from around the world who want a glimpse of polar bears that populate the Churchill area. It also acts as an important link for northern Manitoba.

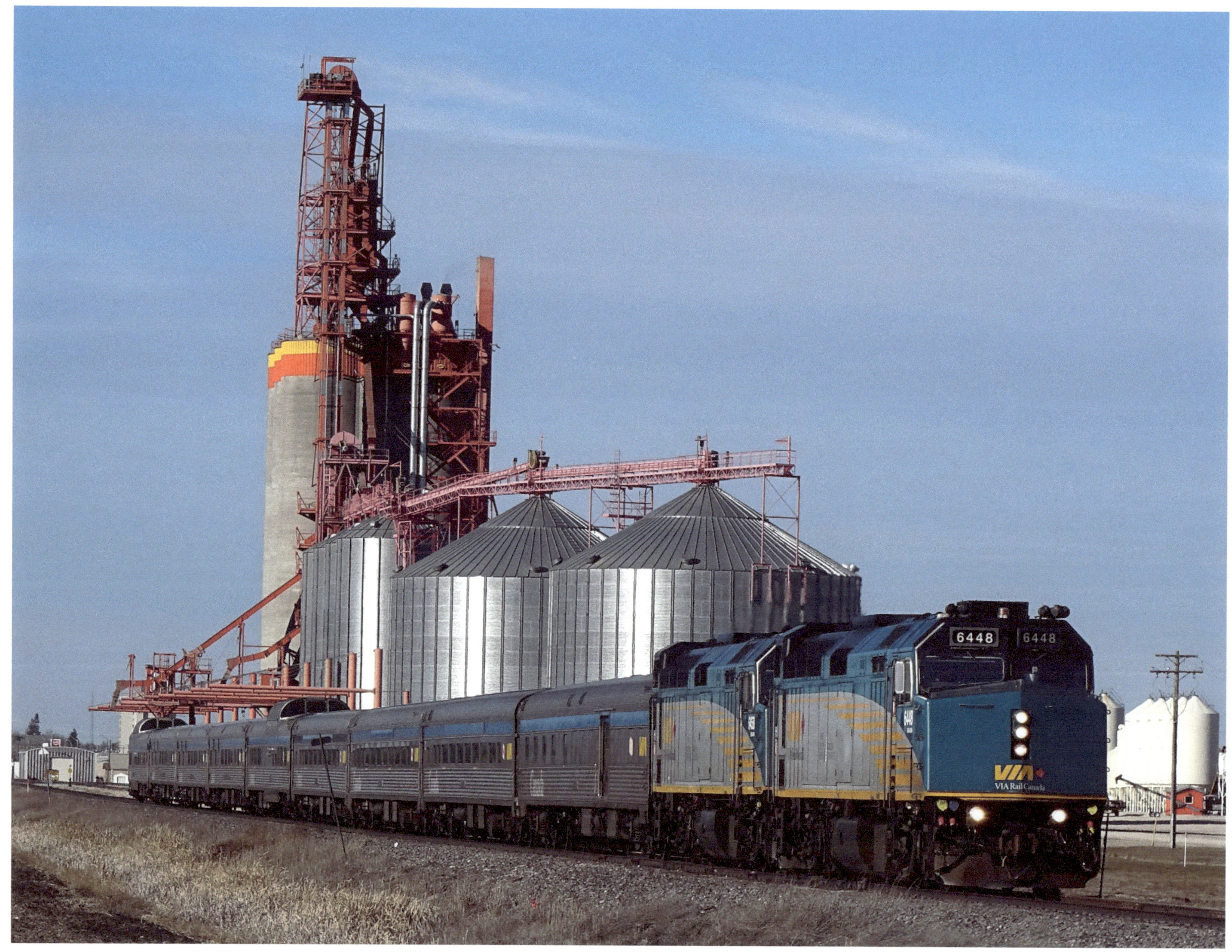

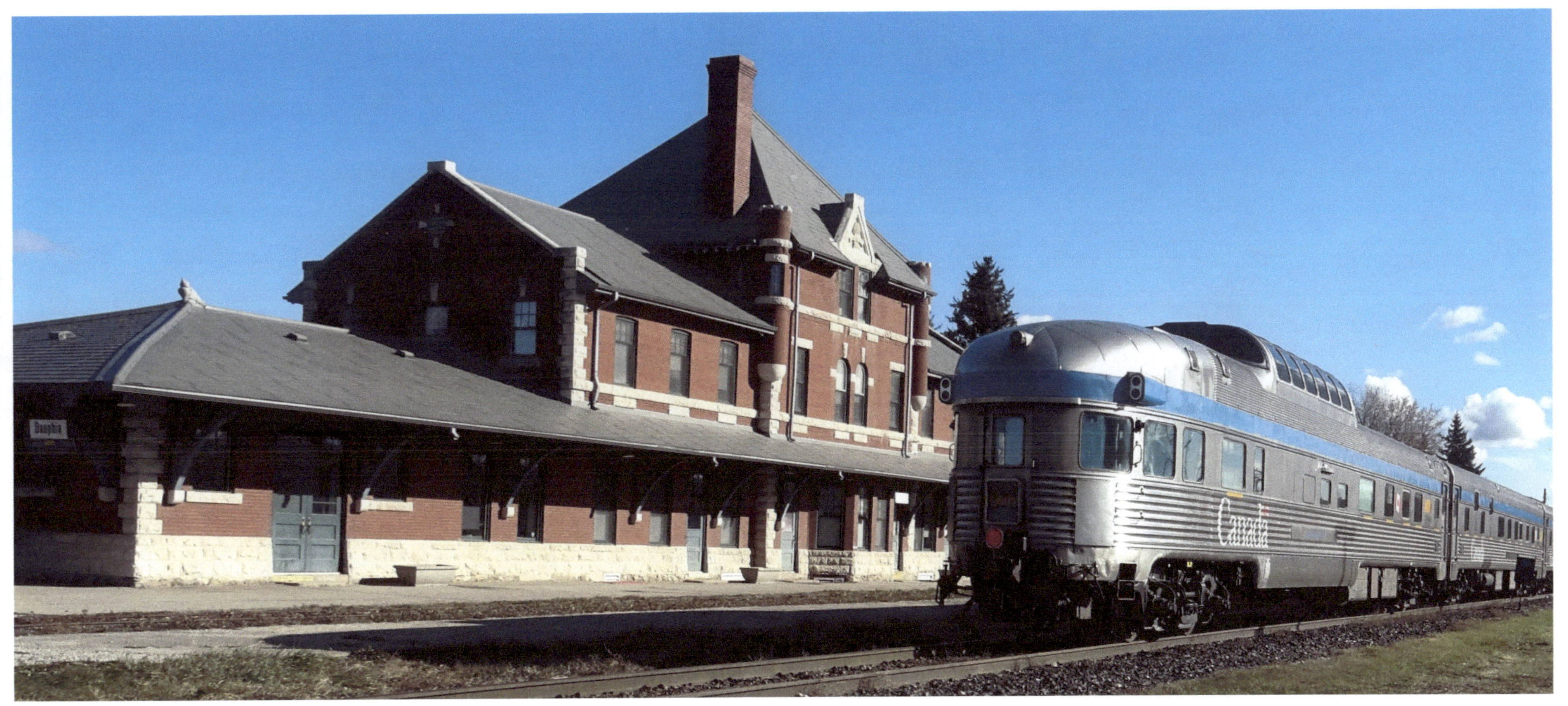

The Churchill train is seen on these pages travelling through Dauphin, Manitoba in the central part of the province. Dauphin continues to serve as a crew change point for Canadian National Railway but VIA crews no longer change here, now running through between Winnipeg and Canora, Saskatchewan. However, the community continues to be a stop for this northern train service.

Dauphin was founded as a village in 1898. Its name dates back to the arrival of French explorer Pierre de La Verendrye during the 1730s. La Verendrye would name a post in the region Dauphin after the eldest son of the King of France Louis XV in 1741.

The Lake Manitoba Railway and Canal Company would build into the area in 1896 and would serve the existing communities of Old Dauphin and Gartmore. Farmers from Ontario had settled in the area in the 1880s and the railway would allow the region to thrive. The Lake Manitoba company would be operated by William Mackenzie and Donald Mann and form the beginnings of the Canadian Northern Railway.

Dauphin would not only become a major agriculture center for new settlers but also a primary railway point for the Canadian Northern. A roundhouse and shop building were built here along with railway yards. Dauphin would be the stepping stone for expansion by the CNR as it extended across Western Canada.

The railway erected a large station in the community that would be completed in 1912 to replace a smaller structure. It is shown above with dome-observation car Tremblant Park passing by. It befit the town's importance to the Canadian Northern. Architect Ralph Pratt is credited with designing the station and also a number of other Canadian Northern buildings.

During World War II Dauphin would be home to two Commonwealth Air Training Plan bases and would host airmen from around the world. Many of the military personnel became extended members of the Dauphin community and the town was well remembered for the hospitality it provided.

Dauphin's continued importance to agriculture is shown at left with VIA 692 passing the recently completed Richardson Pioneer grain terminal located on the east side of the community. This grain elevator has a capacity for over 27000 tons of grain and serves a large area.

The CN station building was designated under the Heritage Railway Stations Protection Act in 1990. It was restored with government funding becoming home to offices and a museum in the early 2000s. The building has become a showpiece of the community.

26

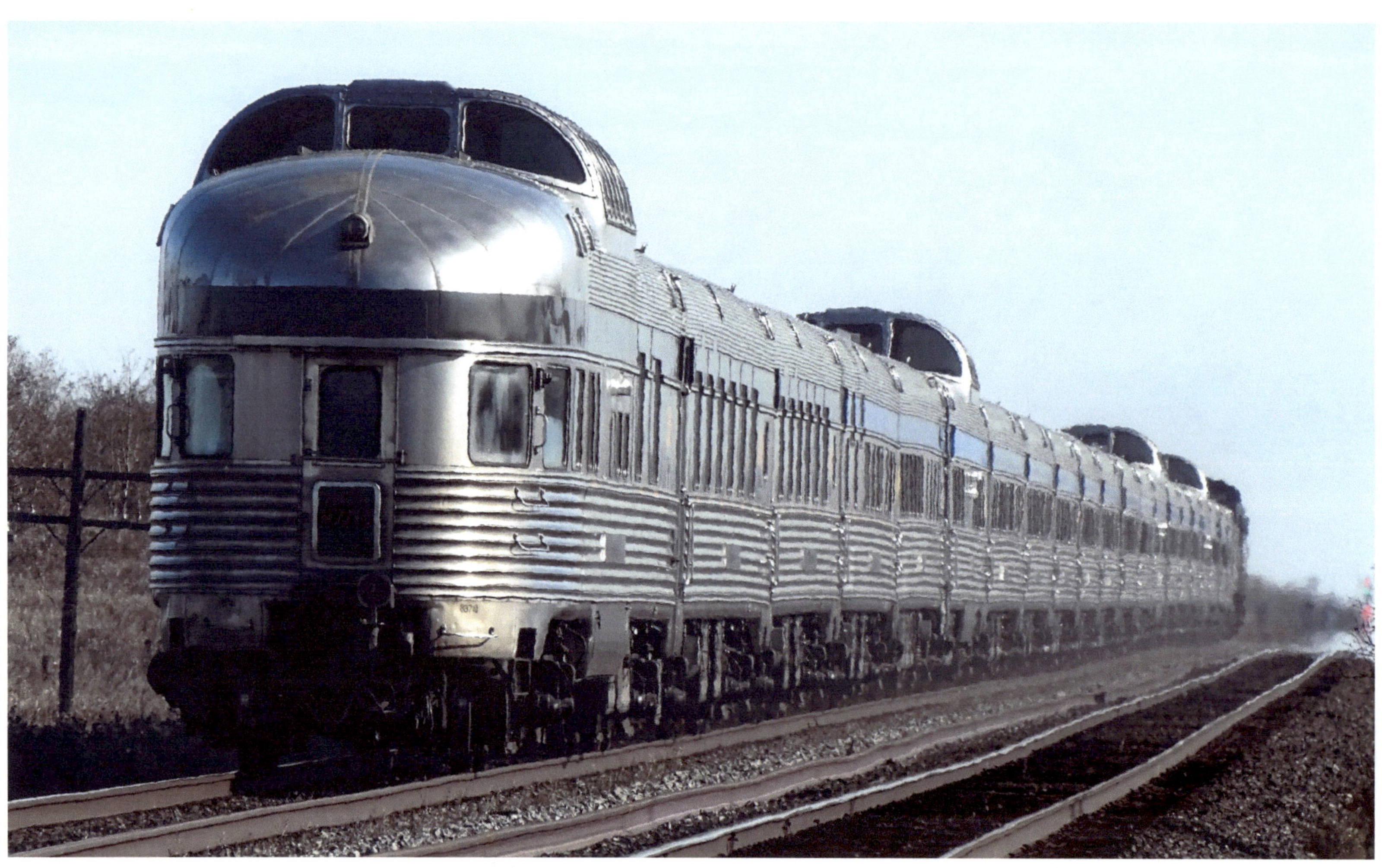